Dear Barb: Answers to Your Everyday Questions

Barbara Godin

Published by BARBARA GODIN, 2020.

While every precaution has been taken in the preparation of this book, the publisher assumes no responsibility for errors or omissions, or for damages resulting from the use of the information contained herein.

DEAR BARB: ANSWERS TO YOUR EVERYDAY QUESTIONS

First edition. August 31, 2020.

Copyright © 2020 Barbara Godin.

ISBN: 978-1927710463

Written by Barbara Godin.

About This Book

This book is a collection of more than 90 *"Dear Barb"* columns. These articles were chosen from more than 500 published columns from 2003 to 2020. *"Dear Barb"* addresses questions covering a variety of everyday issues we all face. This is the first of two books featuring *"Dear Barb"* columns.

Part 1 - FAMILY - "Other things may change us, but we start and end with the family." – Anthony Brandt

INTRUSIVE MOTHER-IN-LAW

DEAR BARB:

My husband and I have been married for ten years and we have three young children. We live fairly close to my husband's parents, so they have been quite involved with our family life. My problem is with my mother-in-law. I have always struggled to get along with her, but as she's getting older, she is becoming more intrusive in our lives, and I am fed up with it. My husband and I are arguing all the time about her. He needs to tell her to stay out of our lives, but he says if I feel that way then I should tell her. Even the kids are complaining about her, as she is always asking them where they are going and what they are doing. If she doesn't think they should go somewhere she will tell me or my husband that we should not allow them to go to such and such a place.

I feel she is undermining us as parents. Through the years she has helped a lot with the kids and I really do appreciate that, but now they are more independent it almost seems like she is trying to keep them from growing up. I feel so alone in this situation; my husband is not supporting me at all. Do you have any advice or suggestions on how I can deal with this, or get my husband more involved? Thanks, Sara.

• • • •

HI SARA:

Thanks for writing. I'm sure there are many daughters-in-law who are going through similar scenarios to what you are experiencing. Mothers-in-law can be difficult and often believe no one is good enough for their son. Frequently mothers do not want to relinquish control of their sons to another woman. Their attempts to control their daughters-in-law are an indirect way of maintaining some level of control over their sons. As well, it is common for mothers-in-law to meddle in the way couples parent their children—another way to maintain a place in their sons' lives.

There are ways you and your husband can prevent this from causing problems in your marriage. First, you and your husband need to set boundaries and follow through on these boundaries. Your husband probably feels caught in the middle, but he needs to support you, rather than side with his mother. You are a family unit and you both have to agree on how you are going to raise your children and take care of your household. Your mother-in-law is the grandmother and should not be deciding how you will raise your children. Your mother-in-law's role should be as a supportive, loving grandmother to your children. I hope this information is helpful. Good Luck Sara.

HUSBAND PUTS FAMILY FIRST

DEAR BARB:

My husband and I have been married for eight years and we have two children. We get along well for the most part. Our major problem is that I feel my husband puts his family (mainly his parents) before our children and me. Whenever his mother calls, he drops whatever he's doing and goes to her. When we married, I realized that because he was from an Italian family and I was not, we may have some problems. I'm starting to wonder if I can live with this for the rest of my life. Do you have any advice to help me deal with this? - Anonymous Anywhere

• • • •

DEAR ANONYMOUS:

Thanks for writing. I understand your need for anonymity as this is a very sensitive issue. In-law problems rank as one of the top ten stressors in a marriage. It's too bad that you and your husband couldn't deal with this issue earlier in your marriage, but it's still not too late.

You don't mention how your husband reacts to his family's demands. When he responds to their calls, does he go willingly, or is he just as frustrated as you? Since you are the one who seems to be at her wit's end, I will assume he goes willingly.

First, you have to discuss this with your husband but be gentle and not confrontational. Tell him how you feel, but don't attack his family or his culture or belittle him for being a caring son. These approaches will put him on the defensive and you will get nowhere. Explain to him that you feel less important than his family. Give him a chance to digest what you are telling him. Don't expect everything to change overnight, give him time. When he does something that indicates he is trying to put you ahead of his family, be supportive. Let him know you appreciate his efforts.

I know this will be frustrating for you, but don't expect things to change quickly. Most importantly, pick your battles.

You understand that since he is from an ethnic family, his familial expectations are different than those of Canadian families. Therefore, as hard as it may be, you may have to accept some of this behavior and not see it as diminishing you in any way.

Ultimately, if you try your best and still do not feel you are making any progress, I suggest you find a good marriage counselor. Your marriage is far too important to give up without trying every possible avenue open to you.

Good luck, and don't give up on your marriage. With some work, I trust you and your husband will be able to get through this turmoil and as a result have a better, stronger marriage.

• • • •

LENDING MONEY TO FAMILY

• • • •

DEAR BARB:

My younger brother and I have always been close until he got married three years ago. My husband and I have never gotten along with my sister-in-law. In fact, Melissa seems to have a problem getting along with everyone. Recently Melissa and Jay got into financial difficulties and Jay approached me and my husband about borrowing money. We haven't decided yet whether we will lend it to them.

My concerns are that Melissa will get into an argument with us and use it as an excuse not to pay us back. I'm trying to maintain a relationship with my brother despite his wife, so I'm not sure if we should take a chance and lend them the money.

Either way could lead to problems between us. Not sure what to do. – Anne

• • • •

HI ANNE:

Thanks for sharing your situation. I will try to help you sort it out.

You are in a very delicate situation that is further complicated by the fact that you and your sister-in-law don't get along that well. You didn't say what has caused your brother and his wife to have these financial difficulties. Was it careless spending, or did they lose their jobs? Are there alcohol and drug problems, or other irresponsible behaviours? If either or both have alcohol or drug problems, lending them money will enable them to continue with this destructive behaviour. Therefore, there would be no debating the right thing to do in that situation.

If they have gotten into this position through no fault of their own, then you may have to think carefully about what you want to do. I believe that if you are going to lend money to your family, it's best to be prepared for the possibility that you may not get it back. You don't want money to come between you and your family members.

For example, if you need the money and are expecting to be paid by a certain date and they don't pay, you can be sure your relationship will be affected. You also have to consider your husband's feelings about lending money to your brother and his wife. You don't want to cause strain in your marriage.

If you cannot afford to lose the money, then my advice would be not to lend it. If you decide to lend the money and you get it back, then consider it a bonus. I hope this advice is helpful.

••••

MOM'S TREASURES

••••

DEAR BARB:

My mother is in her mid-seventies and is starting to slow down. My father passed away five years ago and my mom has stayed in our family home. Recently, she decided to move into an apartment and has been getting rid of stuff. The problem is mom expects me and my two sisters to take all her stuff, like dishes, pictures, and numerous mementos. We don't want any of Mom's stuff and when we hinted that we didn't want anything, it was obvious she was hurt. My sisters and I have a million good memories in our hearts, and we don't need any of this stuff.

We don't know how to manage this situation without causing Mom more pain. One of my sisters feels we should just take the stuff and donate it without telling Mom. I don't want to do that because what would we say when mom comes over and doesn't see any of her stuff? We really need some advice. - Thanks, Jessica.

••••

HEY JESSICA:

You are in a difficult position in which many adult children find themselves. The movement today is towards minimalism[1]. I think you and your sisters and your mom need to read the book The Gentle Art of Swedish Death Cleaning[2] by

---

1. https://www.vocabulary.com/dictionary/minimalist

Margareta Magnusson. The book will help your mom to understand the process of letting go and she will come to realize that it is nothing personal.

As well, you and your sisters could go through your mom's stuff and pick out items that are special to each of you and create a memory box. Your memories are not in a set of China or a picture from your great grandma, your memories are in your heart and you need to help your mom to understand how you feel. Perhaps you could spend some time speaking to other family members about whether they would want these items. Also, you can take pictures to preserve the memory, without having to keep the item. Millennials generally do not want to keep large sets of china to use simply for Christmas dinner; they use their everyday dishes. Explain to your mom that you don't want to keep stuff that you will never use.

Although understandably, the boomers want their kids to keep their treasures, it is unfair to expect them to take on stuff that they have no use for. The focus of today's millennials is often on traveling and collecting worldly experiences and memories, rather than accumulating goods to sit in a cabinet or basement. Thanks for your letter, Jessica.

••••

BLENDING FAMILIES

••••

DEAR BARB:

---

2. https://www.familyhandyman.com/smart-homeowner/10-things-to-know-about-swedish-death-cleaning/

My husband and I have been married for two years and we each brought children into the marriage. He has two boys and I have one. His youngest is twelve and is autistic and the other fifteen while my son is eight. We have been having a lot of problems with the three boys getting along. They each have their issues and naturally, we each favor our own children. I find the twelve-year-old very hard to deal with. My husband caters to him and has no expectations for him. He goes to a regular school and functions fairly well; he just seems to have social issues. The oldest is a teen and knows everything. My youngest is a sweet, good-natured boy who wants to hang out with his older brothers, but they aren't very accommodating. My husband is a great guy and when it is just the two of us there are no problems, but when we begin discussing the boys, we end up in an argument.

I don't want this to ruin our marriage, but I don't know what to do. I've suggested family counseling, but my husband says we just need to adjust to each other. Well, it's been two years; I think we're beyond the adjustment phase. Do you have any suggestions on where we can go from here? - Thanks, Laura.

••••

HI LAURA:

Great Question! Blended families are the new norm, and they can and do work, but it takes compromise and understanding from everyone involved. The idea of the Brady Bunch is basically that, an ideal, not a reality. According to the University of Houston, 1300 new stepfamilies are established every day in the USA. A concern for stepfamilies is that the chances of second and third marriages ending in divorce are considerably higher than first marriages. A major reason for this is because of the challenges involved in blended families.

For example, I assume your son was an only child and now he must adjust to having two new brothers, one of which is autistic. Autism can be many things and requires knowledge and adjustment from everyone in the family. You may want to contact autismcanada.org to assist with understanding some questions you and your son may have about Autism. As well, the middle child has now lost his position as the youngest in the family, which changes his view of where he belongs. You can see many issues are going on. It's important that you continue to spend time alone with your son and that your husband spends time with his sons. The children need to know that they still have their place with their biological parents. As well, you need to have family time and set a tradition where you all do things together as a family. Perhaps a movie or game night, or a hike together, find an activity that will help you bond.

You each need to maintain your relationship with your own child/children, and then the relationship with the whole family. It is also important that you and your husband still spend time alone together. It may seem complicated, but it can work, with patience, love, and understanding. I agree that a few visits to a family counselor would be helpful. Good luck with your blended family.

. . . .

ESTRANGED SON

. . . .

DEAR BARB:

My adult son has cut off all ties with me and I am devastated! Since his dad and I divorced my son and I have had issues. There seems to be tension between us, almost like he is blaming me for the divorce. I did choose to leave the marriage, but I don't see how this should have damaged my relationship with my son.

I have tried to contact him and sent him cards, texts, and Christmas and birthday presents, but no response. This has gone on for over a year this time. He had done this to me a couple of times before and each time when we got back together, I tried to find out what the problem was. The last time he told me it had nothing to do with me, it was just things that he had to work out. He said he has now matured and can handle stress better. Obviously, that wasn't the case.

This last blow-up occurred because my son expected me to remove some pictures of his ex-wife on social media and I decided not to because there were other family members in the pictures. My son gave me an ultimatum: if I didn't do it, he wouldn't speak to me again. I didn't believe he would do this over something so trivia, but he did.

I love my son tremendously, but I have been through this so many times with him, and unless I do exactly what he wants, he does this to me. Why would a child do this to a parent? I did not abuse or neglect him in any way. I am finding this very difficult, some days I'm ok and other days it makes me extremely sad. Do you have any advice for a heartbroken mother? Thanks, Anne.

• • • •

HI ANNE:

So sorry to hear about your situation. I have gotten a few letters about similar scenarios. Sometimes people have a hard time dealing with conflict, so rather than face it, they choose to escape. It sounds like your son may be one of them. It is extremely painful when an adult child cuts off contact with a parent, especially a mother. Mothers are always dealing with feelings of guilt and questioning whether they are good mothers, so something like this just magnifies those feelings. Plus, there is the belief that other people will think they must have been a terrible parent for their child to have done this to them.

You have a right to take a stand and make your own choices and decisions, as does your son. If you are not flaunting these pictures by tagging your son, he has to respect your right to put whatever you want on your social media accounts. It seems he doesn't want to see any reminders of his failed marriage but eliminating the pictures does not make the failed marriage disappear. When you feel bad, remember that you did not cut your son out of your life, this was his choice.

Try not to let anger get the best of you. Perhaps at some point, you will be able to have a conversation about what is really bothering your son and you may find out, as he has said before, that it has nothing to do with you. In the meantime, a support group may help you get through this difficult time. Thank you for sharing with our readers.

• • • •

STRESSED MOM

• • • •

DEAR BARB:

I'm a forty-year-old mom of three who is working full-time and taking university courses. Life just seems to be so busy for me;

I never have time to relax. My husband is very laid back and leaves everything to me. I feel like I'm going through the motions of life and not enjoying anything. I was thinking of seeing my doctor to get some tranquilizers to help me relax, but I'm not sure that is the right thing to do. Everyone tells me to just relax, but that's easier said than done!!!

Do you have any suggestions on how I can learn to relax? - Stressed in Calgary.

• • • •

DEAR STRESSED:

I am not surprised that you are stressed as your life is very busy with working full time, going to school, and raising three children. Wow, I'm exhausted just thinking about it! You say your husband is very laid back and that is fine, but he needs to help out. A lot of men are reluctant to take on a task for fear of not doing it the way their wives would like it to be done.

Try making up a schedule where he is responsible for some of the chores and childcare. Suggesting ways he can help out will give him the direction he needs. Discuss your stress levels with your doctor; there may be other options for you besides tranquilizers. You need to learn ways to relax. Join a yoga or meditation class. While you are driving to and from work pop in a relaxation CD, it will calm you and give you quiet breaks during the day. Take care of yourself first, otherwise, your family, marriage, and work will suffer.

• • • •

SIBLING PARENTS

• • • •

DEAR BARB:

My sister and I each have two children. Mine are 10 and 12 and hers are 16 and 18. We have always had different ways of raising them: I am a very protective parent, while my sister is more relaxed. We've had an ongoing debate about whether a parent should shield their children from unpleasant situations.

I think we should try our best to protect our children as long as we can, I feel they will have to face enough hardships when they are adults, and they don't need to begin dealing with these issues as children. But my sister thinks we should let them face whatever comes their way. She thinks it will make them better adults. We were just wondering what your opinion is. – Emily

• • • •

HI EMILY:

We all want to protect our children from the unpleasantness of life, but that is not always the best. Children need to learn the consequences of their actions. If they don't learn when they are young, when they become adults and make bad decisions, as we all do, they may not be able to cope with the negative outcomes. We learn about life through the choices we make, some good and some bad.

If you protect your child from harmful outcomes, they will not have the ability to work through these issues and make healthier decisions next time. Pain is a part of life, and our children need to realize this. As a parent, you can take the time to discuss these struggles with your child and help them develop better ways to manage the ups and downs of life. I don't agree with your sister that we should allow our children to face everything that life throws at them.

As parents, we can help our children deal with age-appropriate situations. Encouragement and support are the best way to educate our children about the ups and downs of life. Thanks for writing Emily.

· · · ·

SISTER'S BOYFRIENDS NUMEROUS

· · · ·

DEAR BARB:

Well, another Thanksgiving has been ruined because of my sister! She is divorced and has two kids. For the last three Thanksgivings, she has brought a different guy and his kids to our family dinner. She hardly knows these guys, so everyone feels uncomfortable. The guy she brought this year had three kids. Two were in their early teens. The youngest one was running through the house making a mess and not listening to anyone while his father ignored him. My sister tried to get the boy to listen, but he completely disregarded what she said. Even Mom stepped in and tried to control him, to no avail. Meanwhile, the teenagers were on their phones for the most part, except when I caught the older one smoking weed outside. I laid into him about doing something illegal at my mom's house. At least he listened to me.

We don't know what to do about this. My brother and I want my sister and her kids to share family events, but why does she always have to bring these guys that she hardly knows, plus their kids? Do you have any suggestions on how we could handle this without my sister becoming angry and not showing up? She is a very reactive person. Thanks, Nicole.

• • • •

HI NICOLE:

Sorry to hear about your Thanksgiving, but I think this happens more often than most people realize, especially as people are now having multiple marriages and blended families. Maybe it's time to begin some new family traditions. For example, drag out some old board games and get everyone involved. Get outside and throw a ball around or go for a hike. Get the kids to burn off some energy while creating a fun day they will remember.

This will give mom time to tend to the dinner, or if mom wants to join in the fun, get someone else to peel the potatoes, or just leave the potatoes for a few minutes, while everyone goes for a hike. Kids always function better in a structured environment. Also participating in these activities will allow everyone to get to know each other.

You and your brother could also suggest to your sister that she not bring anyone over until she knows them a little better. Discuss with her how the situation is uncomfortable for everyone. You will have to be careful how to approach this with your sister, as she may get her back up and decide she is not going to attend. You and your brother probably have a pretty good idea of how your sister will react, so consider how you want to proceed. The answer may be to simply keep everyone busy to keep the tension to a minimum.

• • • •

ACCEPT THE CHILD YOU HAVE

••••

DEAR BARB:

I am the mother of a fourteen-year-old daughter. We have always had a strained relationship and it just seems to be getting worse. I had a difficult relationship with my mother, and I hoped that my relationship with my daughter would be better, but it doesn't seem to be. I come from a family of quiet, conservative people, who try hard to be humble for what we have or can do. My family always cautioned me about trying to be "too big for my britches". My daughter is extremely outgoing, always wanting to be the center of attention and the life of the party. She seems to be craving my approval but that is not something I'm comfortable giving.

While I enjoy the fact that she is outgoing, I find myself a bit uncomfortable with it and often try to suppress her. We get into some pretty heated battles which make me feel awful afterward. My husband is much more easygoing and gets along quite well with our daughter. I love my daughter tremendously, but I fear if I don't try to curtail her personality other people will and that will be very painful for her. She is constantly accusing me of trying to change her. I'm really just trying to make her a better person. Looking for some advice. Thanks for your help. - Heather

••••

HI HEATHER:

Thanks for sharing your story. The best advice I can give you is to love the child you have, not the one you wish you had.

You seem to have expectations for your daughter based on your family history. She is an individual. We are not all cut from the same cloth just because we come from the same gene pool. Step out of your comfort zone and embrace your daughter's differences. Throughout her life, she will encounter people who do not appreciate her personality and others who think she's awesome. It's not up to you to "curtail" her personality; your job is to accept her as she is. Fourteen is an age when she is still learning who she is.

You can help her on this journey, not by trying to change her, but rather through acceptance and love. As a parent, your responsibility is to encourage your child to be who they want to be, not who you think they should be. Maybe you can take some cues from your husband and just relax and enjoy your daughter for who she is.

Good luck and remember that the teenage years are challenging for all parents.

....

CARING FOR AN AGING MOTHER

....

DEAR BARB:

My mother has been struggling with heart failure for years and recently took a turn for the worse. She can't do much of anything. I am the only one of her children that lives nearby so the responsibility for her care is falling on me. I'm okay with that, but my husband is not supportive.

We have two teenage children at home, and I'd like him to help prepare meals and take care of the household chores while I am caring for my mother, but he doesn't think that's his job. When I get home from preparing my mom's dinner, my husband expects me to cook dinner for the family. If I try to talk to him about helping, he says he works all day and shouldn't have to come home and make his own dinner! He says since I only work part-time, I should still be able to do everything, plus take care of my mom. I suggested moving my mom in with us, that way it will be easier for me as I will be able to keep an eye on mom while doing my chores around the house. My husband will not even consider having my mom move in, he says we need our space and he's never really got along that well with Mom. My husband is not a bad guy really, but he just likes things the way they are and doesn't adapt well to change. How can I care for my mom and my family and still maintain a good healthy marriage? Thanks for your help. – Kathy

• • • •

HI KATHY:

You are part of the all-too-common sandwich generation, which means being sandwiched between caring for aging parents and your own family. The stress of caring for aging or sick parents is difficult and takes a toll on the caregiver and their family. You need a support system, someone you can vent and share your feelings with, as it doesn't seem your husband can provide this. Try to find another outlet, perhaps a support group in your area. You can check online or ask your physician about local groups. If possible, bring in some outside help to assist with either the care of your mother or help with your own household. Also, you can investigate employing a service to prepare meals for your family as well as your mother. However, this may not be something you can afford.

With two teenagers at home, you could assign them chores and give them a small allowance. Teens always want money. Your husband needs to move into the twenty-first century and adjust to the new normal. It would be nice if things always remained the same, but that's not realistic. As people get older, things happen and health fails. It's an unavoidable part of life. Have a family discussion with your husband and children about pitching in and helping. Maybe your husband could cook every other night and your children could do the cleanup, which will give you some time to do laundry or other chores. A family discussion is the best place to start. I'm sure you can come to a compromise and work this out. Best of luck Kathy.

• • • •

STRESSING ABOUT EASTER GATHERING

• • • •

DEAR BARB:

This may seem like a trivial thing to write an advice column about, but I am totally stressed out. Easter is just around the corner and I'm hosting the family dinner this year. My parents are getting older, so my sisters and I have decided to take turns. I was planning on preparing a ham dinner, but one of my sisters says she won't eat ham. This is news to me since she always ate it in the past.

I wanted everyone to enjoy their dinner, so I then suggested a pork roast. Well, my brother-in-law doesn't like pork. I don't want to cook a turkey since we had turkey for Christmas dinner. So, it seems like I'm left with lamb or roast beef. I know my dad doesn't care for lamb, but he would never complain. Aside from the dinner problems, two of my brothers-in-law are not getting along with each other. It seems one bought a new vehicle and the other one has his nose out of joint about it. I just feel like taking my parents out for dinner and forgetting about everyone else, but I know they want us all to be together. Please help before I go crazy!
- Alisha

• • • •

HI ALISHA:

I don't think your situation is trivial. I think many people are feeling the same way you do right now. These are the exact reasons many people do not enjoy holidays. Experiencing stressful family gatherings while growing up will cause feelings that carry on into adulthood and ruin many special occasions. For many people, the anxiety begins weeks before the occasion as they anticipate things that may occur. It's likely that in many situations, the anticipation causes more stress than the actual event.

If you are hosting the family dinner, then I think it is up to you to decide what you want to prepare. If your last meal was turkey, then I can see why you would not want to prepare it again. You are never going to be able to please everyone. Hopefully, you can present enough of a variety of foods that each person will find something they like.

As for the relationship problems between your brothers-in-law, I would suggest you try to ignore them. Your job is to bring the family together for a nice meal. How they choose to interact with each other is beyond your control.

Happy Easter, Alisha, and try to look at the bigger picture: that your family is together and that your parents are still able to share the day with all of you.

• • • •

GRANDMOTHER IS MOVING ON

• • • •

DEAR BARB:

I lost my husband two years ago. It was a very difficult time in my life. I was quite lonely and as a result, I began spending a lot of time with my grandchildren, babysitting, etc. Recently I met a widower, and we are spending time together. My son is getting upset that I am not always available to babysit or drive the kids around as frequently as I used to. He is making me feel guilty because I am spending time with this gentleman.

My grandkids are getting older, developing their own lives with friends as well, and becoming involved in many sports activities. I still want to be involved with my grandchildren, but shouldn't I be entitled to have a life of my own life? I was hoping I could have my son read your response to help him understand how I feel. – Irene

• • • •

DEAR IRENE:

Great question. I'm sure many grandparents are in similar situations. Your son has probably gotten accustomed to the ease of just phoning up mom when he needed a babysitter.

Now he can't do that. He will not only have to make other arrangements but most likely will have to pay someone, which he may or may not have done with you.

You do not need to feel guilty. Everyone is entitled to live their own life to the fullest. You have fulfilled your obligation to raise your children and now it's their turn to raise their own children. Not to say you shouldn't babysit, but it should be at your convenience. A lot of grandparents make the decision early on that they will not babysit grandchildren. They don't want to take on that role. You chose to babysit, as it probably helped you in your grief while helping your son as well.

The bond between grandparents and their grandchildren is a special one and should be honored. You can maintain that relationship without having to babysit. Perhaps you can include your new friend in some activities with your grandchildren. Depending on whether he has grandchildren or not, this could be an enjoyable, fun activity you can share.

I think you should discuss your feelings with your son and if you feel it's necessary, give him this column to read. It may take a while for him to come around, but ultimately if he wants you to be happy, he will understand.

• • • •

A MARRIAGE OF THREE

• • • •

DEAR BARB:

I hope you can help me with my problem. My sister-in-law is driving me crazy. Steve and I have been married for over 20 years. Steve's father died when Steve was quite young, and his mother and older sister raised him. His sister never married but ended up taking care of the mother until her death.

Steve's mother and sister have always been a big part of our lives, but things changed drastically a couple of years ago when the mother passed away. Now Steve's sister calls or comes over every day. These are not brief visits. When she calls, she talks to Steve for hours on the phone, asking him questions about every aspect of our lives. I've tried to talk to Steve about the fact that I don't want his sister to know everything about us. He doesn't understand but gets angry and says that I don't like his sister. It's not that I don't like her, but I feel like there are three of us in our marriage. I don't mind him having a relationship with his sister, but this is just too much. What can I do? – Patty

• • • •

HI PATTY:

In-laws can be a pain, as you know, but they are a part of our lives that we cannot avoid.

You are in a delicate situation, as is your husband, who most likely is feeling sandwiched between the two women in his life. He may feel more of an obligation to his sister than most brothers because she was the one who raised him and took care of his mother, ultimately allowing him to have a life of his own.

It appears your sister-in-law does not have much of a life. Perhaps you and your husband could encourage her to become involved in activities where she would meet other people. I imagine your husband is exhausted from having to deal with his sister on the phone or at your home for extended periods, consequently not leaving him with much time for you.

Unfortunately, I don't think you will be able to resolve this without outside assistance. Your husband feels you don't want him to have a relationship with his sister, but you state this is not the case. I believe you just want to be a priority, which you should be as his wife. Moreover, I believe your husband is trying his best to make everyone happy and keep the peace, but he is not able to achieve this.

I would recommend that you discuss this situation with your family doctor, who will be able to refer you to a professional counselor. I feel confident you will be able to establish some boundaries and work this situation out to everyone's satisfaction. Thanks for writing.

• • • •

SISTER IS MENTALLY ILL

• • • •

DEAR BARB:

My sister suffers from mental illness and no matter what I do to try to help her she resists. She barely eats and is just skin and bones. She takes a lot of prescription drugs and says her problems are all a result of her nerves. Her doctor does nothing to help her, other than giving her more drugs. He does not seem to see that she is mentally ill, as she is very good at masking her illness.

I cannot understand why she does not want to help herself. Our family has tried to do whatever we can, but she always ends up getting angry and attempts to alienate us. Even her children do not want to see her as they can't deal with her unstable moods and fits of rage. I'm ready to give up too, but I'm having a hard time letting go. What should I do? – Kevin

HEY KEVIN:

You sound like a caring brother. Without a doubt, it is very difficult to deal with individuals who are suffering from mental illness. Part of their illness is that they don't see themselves as ill. Your view of the world is coming from a completely different place than your sister's. The rights of the mentally ill allow them to maintain their freedom unless they are suicidal or homicidal.

Consequently, there is nothing you can do until your sister is ready to accept your help. As hard as it is, try to be there for her as much as she will allow, other than that your hands are tied. Best of luck Kevin.

DAUGHTER IS NOT WILLING TO SHARE

DEAR BARB:

I married my ex when we were both quite young. Even though our relationship was difficult we tried our best to stay together for our daughter. Eventually, it got to the point that we were arguing constantly, and we felt it wasn't the best atmosphere to raise our daughter. We separated when Melanie was nine years old. My ex met someone right away and Melanie didn't like her, but since she didn't live with her dad, it wasn't a big trauma for her. My ex spends time alone with our daughter and that seems to be working out.

Fast forward a few years and Melanie is now a teenager and I have begun dating. I wasn't interested in seeing anyone for quite a while, but recently I met this guy at work, and we just clicked. When Melanie got wind of the situation she freaked! She does not want me to see anyone. Her reaction was similar to the way it was when her dad began dating his girlfriend. Since Melanie lives with me most of the time, I cannot do what her dad has done, and not include my new guy in our lives.

I am not sure how to handle this situation. I love my daughter and want her to be happy, but I really like this guy. He's very understanding and knows that I must put my daughter first. I don't know what to do now. Looking for some advice. Thanks, Heather.

• • • •

HEY HEATHER:

Good question! First, I would like to say having a teenager has its challenges, add divorce and new relationships and you have a very difficult situation. It is important not to rush things. Allow your daughter to slowly get used to your boyfriend. Take time to get to know this person and make sure he is someone that you want to introduce to your daughter. You did say he's very understanding, but you didn't say whether he has children. That may add another dimension to the mix. Your daughter will have a whole new family to adjust to.

Begin with short visits, maybe the three of you going to a place of your daughter's choosing. That way she will feel she has some input and is still important. It is essential not to spend a lot of time away from home with the new person initially as this may cause resentment toward your daughter. Try to manage your time with him, while your daughter is visiting her dad.

As your relationship progresses reassure your daughter that you are not replacing her father, he will always be her father. If your daughter is not willing to open up and accept someone new into your life, then I would suggest you and your daughter seek some professional counseling to help with the adjustment phase. Take it slow, Heather - one step at a time.

. . . .

MOM'S BACK

. . . .

DEAR BARB:

I am a forty-year-old mother of three. I had a rough upbringing as my mother was very neglectful and gave me away to relatives. I haven't seen her for years and now she wants to become a part of my life and see her grandchildren. I don't know if I can forgive her, however, my children want to meet their grandmother. I have never talked much about my mom to my kids, so they don't know a lot about her, and they are still young.

I am happy in my life and hesitant to allow my mom back into my life for fear of being hurt again. What do you think I should do? - Help, Hanna.

. . . .

HI HANNA:

You seem to have gotten over your dysfunctional upbringing and found happiness in your life, a feat that many people are not able to accomplish. I think you owe it to yourself, your children, and your mother to give your mother a second chance. She may have worked through a lot of the issues that caused her to do the things she did, and now she wants an opportunity to make it up to you and her grandchildren.

If you try and you are not able to let the past go, at least you will know that you have tried and have given your children an opportunity to meet their grandmother. Thanks for your question, Hanna.

• • • •

DYSFUNCTIONAL REUNION

• • • •

DEAR BARB:

I grew up in a somewhat dysfunctional family. My parents divorced when we were all quite young, and the divorce was angry and bitter. This bitterness became a part of our household and our relationships with each other. As soon as we were able to we left home and rarely spoke to each other for many years. As an adult, I am trying to turn the family dynamics around and bring my family together. I have been arranging a family get-together every year for the past four years, as well as the occasional dinner at Christmas or other special occasions. The problem is no one reciprocates.

When I arrange these events some family members show up, but no one else ever takes the initiative to make arrangements for next time. When we have the yearly reunion at a park or campground, the families each stay with their own family members. I have tried to organize things like games for the kids, but no one else gets involved. They all just sit there talking with their family members, while I take care of the kids. When I post the date on Facebook for the get-together everyone seems excited about it, but when we get there it's totally different.

Am I beating a dead horse? It almost seems like it's too late to bring this family together. Should I just give up? – Maria

• • • •

HI MARIA:

Thanks for sharing. Unfortunately, there always seems to be one or two people in a family who do all the social planning and when they get tired of doing it, the get-togethers stop. So, I guess it's up to you if you want to continue arranging these gatherings. If you stop it is possible someone else will eventually start arranging them, but you won't know that until you do it.

If you are finding that you don't want to do this anymore (it is a lot of work, after all) then you could always get together with the family members you choose to. That way you can keep in contact with the relatives you want to and who reciprocate your invitations. Bringing a family back together after a long estrangement is difficult and requires a lot of forgiveness and acceptance, and it can only be successful if all parties want it. I found some information online about coping with estranged family relationships at https://tinybuddha.com/blog/how-to-cope-with-a-toxic-family-relationship/

I also found a quote on this page that I like:

"Letting go doesn't mean giving up, but rather accepting that there are things that cannot be." Unknown

• • • •

SAYING FAREWELL TO DAD

••••

DEAR BARB:

I am a part-time student and the mother of three young children. My father is in the final stages of colon cancer and he and my mom are struggling. I have always been close to my parents, but my brother hasn't. For the most part, he has been estranged from the family. My parents have tried to resolve issues with him, but he always finds something wrong with how they treated him, or the choices that they have made with which he didn't agree. He hasn't spoken to my parents for the last five years.

I want him to visit my dad before he passes, but whenever I bring up the topic, he tells me it's none of my business and shuts me down. I think he is going to regret not making peace with my dad after he's gone. Am I wrong in trying to get them to reconcile? Should I just let things be? - Looking for advice. – Brenda

••••

HI BRENDA:

Sorry your family is facing this traumatic issue. Unfortunately, there is nothing you can do about it. If you try to force your brother to make amends with your dad when he doesn't want to, it will only cause dissension between you and your brother. In life, we all make our own choices and have to live with the consequences. You can't control what your brother chooses to do.

My advice would be to let this be. Thanks for your letter.

••••

TIME TO TURN THE PAGE

• • • •

DEAR BARB:

Hi, I have been reading your column almost weekly and I finally decided to write. For most of my life, I have been an angry, some say vindictive person. I don't feel I have been treated well by my family and because of my anger, I rarely see them. None of them seem to listen to what I say or care how I feel. Even though I miss them, I can't seem to put the anger away and have a relationship with them. I know there are a lot of people who have been treated worse than I have and can maintain ties with their families, but I just can't seem to let go. It's not like I was abused or neglected, I just didn't like some of the things family members did.

For example, my sister kept a wedding picture of me and my ex-husband on her Instagram and wouldn't take it down when asked, so I haven't spoken to her since. I'm wondering if maybe I overreacted. I don't want to hang on to this anger, but I can't make peace with it. I also don't speak to my brother or my mother. They have attempted to contact me, but I don't know how to respond, so I just don't say anything.

I can't seem to admit that maybe I was wrong. Looking for suggestions on how I can move forward and let go of this anger. - Lonely in PEI.

• • • •

HEY LONELY:

Thanks for your letter. You know that it's time to make some changes in your life, as this is not the way you want to live. When you think about it, do you think it is worth not speaking to your sister or family members because of an Instagram picture, or because they don't manage their life the way you think they should? These are not good reasons to cut ties with your family. This estrangement could go on for years unless you change it. What happened between you and your ex-husband has nothing to do with your sister. It is her choice to keep the picture up or take it down.

You really can't control what other people do. You may not like what they do, but that is their choice, not yours. Life is all about making choices. If you truly want to let go of the anger, you must choose a different response. Maybe your sister didn't want to be told what to do. So, yes, I do think you are overreacting. Moving on to a more fulfilling life includes accepting the things you cannot change.

I would suggest you investigate some counseling or meditation to help you come to terms with your anger. I am sure that your letter will resonate with others in similar situations. I believe this is the first step on the road to change.

• • • •

WONDERING WHERE I BELONG

• • • •

DEAR BARB:

I am in my early twenties and just found out I was adopted. I had a very happy childhood and felt loved by my parents, but since I never looked like anybody in the family, I felt different. In the back of my mind, I wondered if I was adopted because I was so dark and both my parents were fair, but I just put it out of my mind. Despite my suspicions, I was shocked when my parents sat me down and told me. They felt it was best that I didn't know until I was old enough to deal with it. I can't say I agree with that. I think it would have been better if I knew and grew up knowing the truth.

This revelation just put my whole world into chaos! Also, when my parents told me I was adopted, they presented me with my birth parents' names and contact information. Apparently, they have kept in touch with them through the years, even sending pictures to them. My parents said it is up to me if I want to contact my biological parents and they said they would support whatever I decide to do.

I am so confused I don't know what I should do. I feel that since my birth parents gave me away, why would I want to reconnect with them? On the other hand, I'm curious, and if I have siblings, I would want to meet them. I love my adopted parents, but I am kind of angry that they held this information from me for all these years, especially since they were in contact with my biological parents. I just feel totally confused! - Sally

• • • •

HI SALLY:

Thank you for writing and sharing your story. I'm sure many people have, and are, feeling what you are feeling. I completely understand your confusion; your whole world has been turned upside down. Some parents choose to tell their children that they are adopted from a young age and others decide to wait, as your parents did. Your feelings of abandonment by your birth parents are normal, but you may want to find out why they chose to give you up for adoption. Because they kept in touch with your adoptive parents, they did not want to simply abandon you. Perhaps they felt they were not capable of providing you with a good home and wanted to allow you to have a good life.

Undoubtedly it is a difficult and painful process for a birth mother to go through. You don't know the circumstances of your birth and surrender, but you will never know the truth unless you take a chance and meet your birth family. Perhaps you should join a support group in your area for adoptees who are reuniting with birth parents. Your family doctor will be able to provide information on support groups and you can also check online for more information. Good luck Sally.

• • • •

MEETING BIRTH FAMILY

• • • •

DEAR BARB:

I hate to be focusing on this with what's happening in the world with the global pandemic, but, well, life goes on. I was adopted at 6 months old by a fantastic family. I have always been well cared for and loved, but I felt like there was a void in my life. I never looked like anyone in the family. My adoptive parents had been married for many years and were unable to have children when they adopted me. They eventually had three children of their own. They told me stories of how they had chosen me and that I was special to them, but I felt if they had waited longer, they would have had their own children and wouldn't have adopted me.

In my teens, I began to think about finding my biological parents or siblings. By the time I was in my twenties, I decided I would seriously pursue it. I told my adoptive parents, and they were completely supportive and provided me with as much information as they could. That was two years ago, and I have recently found my birth parents, who are now married with two other children. We have spoken on the phone about arranging a meeting. They seem excited and anxious to meet me; however, I'm a little apprehensive. After all, they got married and had a family and never pursued finding me, which makes me wonder how receptive they are.

Do you think I should meet them? Do you have any suggestions on the best way to handle the initial meeting? I am so filled with anxiety!! Thanks, Wendy.

• • • •

HI WENDY:

Thanks for your letter and you are right; despite this horrible situation, life does go on and people still have issues to work through. You are at an important crossroads in your life. As you say, even though your adoptive parents loved you and chose you, you still felt a void and for that reason, I would say that you need to meet your biological parents. Some adoptees never feel that void and are perfectly content without ever meeting their biological parents, but I think it is important for you to resolve this.

I will caution you to prepare yourself for the meeting, as these meetings do not always go as we envision. You already appear to have some resentment because your biological parents never looked for you, and you will need to address that.

Perhaps some counseling with someone knowledgeable in these types of meetings would be a beneficial place to begin. Speak with your family doctor about where these services are available in your community. Also, Origins Canada offers some insight into what you can expect from a reunion with your biological family[3]. Good luck Wendy and keep an open mind.

---

3. https://www.originscanada.org/services/adoption-reunion/stages-of-reunion/

Part 2 - ADDICTION - "The journey of a thousand miles begins with one step." - Lao Tzu

••••

MY PARENTS WANT TO KEEP MY DAUGHTER

••••

DEAR BARB:

I am in my early thirties, and I recently completed a methadone program due to my addiction to painkillers. During my years of drug addiction, my parents had been raising my daughter and now they won't give her back to me. I am thankful they were there to care for Paige, but I want her back and I feel I'm capable of taking care of her. I don't want to have problems with my parents, and I don't think it would be good for my daughter to just take her from her grandparents, as she is very attached to them.

I want to do what's best for my daughter, but I am not sure how to handle this situation while keeping everyone happy. – Amanda

••••

HI AMANDA:

Congrats to you on completing your methadone program!

You were fortunate to have your parents care for your daughter rather than CAS taking her into care, as you would have had a difficult time getting her back. Your parents may be fearful you will relapse, and their granddaughter will have to go through the trauma of losing her mother again. I agree it is not in the best interest of your daughter to just take her away from your parents, however, if they do not have legal custody you could take her back and there is nothing, they could do about it.

A gradual transition from grandparents to mom will give everyone time to adjust. Your parents will eventually be confident that you will be able to take care of your daughter when you have her back full-time. Good Luck with this new phase in your life.

••••

ROOMMATE HAS A DRUG PROBLEM

••••

DEAR BARB:

I am in my second year of college. I always thought I was fortunate to find a roommate that I got along well with. However, this year I have noticed a change in my roommate. His grades are falling, he spends a lot of time alone, and he is constantly borrowing money from me that he does not pay back.

I think he may be using drugs, especially oxy cotton. I had never heard of this stuff before. Do you know anything about this drug? If so, what can I do to help my friend realize what he's doing to his life? - Randy

••••

HEY RANDY:

If your roommate is using oxy cotton, he has a serious problem that will require professional help to overcome.

Oxy cotton, or Oxycontin, has been around since the mid-1990s. It is an effective pain reliever that works when other pain relievers fail, such as in the case of cancer patients. It has been referred to as "hillbilly heroin," since initially it was used in rural areas. Eventually, the rest of the world became aware of its powerful effects.

Oxycontin is an opiate; therefore, its addictive qualities are as difficult to overcome as those of heroin. With continued use, a person will develop a tolerance and subsequently require more of the drug to achieve the same high. I think you can see where this problem could lead. A person will sacrifice family, friends, work, or whatever they need to find a means to obtain more of this drug.

Information collected through the Drug Abuse Warning Network[4] indicates how widespread this problem has become as the number of Oxycontin-related emergency room admissions rose from 3,290 in 1996 to 37,393 in 2002.

If you believe your roommate is involved with this drug, you need to seek the help of a trained counselor. They will be able to assist you in approaching your roommate and obtaining the help for him that he needs.

I hope this information is helpful.

• • • •

MY BROTHER IS AN ADDICT

---

[4]. http://dawninfo.samhsa.gov/

DEAR BARB:

Hi, my brother is addicted to opiates. His wife and two kids have suffered extensively from his addiction, as have my parents. He has tried many times to get off the drugs, but it hasn't worked. He is mostly homeless and has no income to speak of. He often shows up at my parent's house in the middle of the night trying to get money. It's so hard for them to say no, even though they have been told by counselors that saying no is the right thing to do. If they give him money, he buys drugs.

I think my brother needs to be in a treatment facility, but he refuses. He says he has some friends who are on methadone, and they have been successful in getting off drugs. To me, it sounds like he is trading one addiction for another. I believe the only way to get clean is to get off all drugs. How can I get my brother into treatment? Another problem is that my brother does not have money and as a family, we are just scraping by. Are there any treatment facilities that are covered by medical insurance? Thanks for your help. – Stephanie

HI STEPHANIE:

So sorry your family is going through this all-too-common scenario. Unfortunately, you cannot force your brother into treatment; he must be ready and willing to accept help. There are insurance-covered treatment centers, but not nearly enough of them. Also, there are guidelines an addict must follow before he will be accepted into treatment. The intention is for the person to be sober and serious about treatment. These services will help the addict get into a medically supervised detox unit to get sober. Once this is accomplished, an appointment with a counselor will be set up and the person will be put on a waitlist until space becomes available. During this time, the addict will be expected to attend meetings and outpatient therapy to maintain sobriety. Unfortunately, many people relapse during this waiting period.

Methadone has some value in the treatment of opiate addiction. It is meant for short-term treatment while people are waiting to get into counseling and treatment to learn to better understand their addiction and why they are vulnerable to it. Methadone alleviates the uncomfortable physical withdrawal symptoms of opiates. Unfortunately, some people end up staying on Methadone for long periods, sometimes even years, thus avoiding dealing with their addiction issues. Ultimately, they become addicted to Methadone. While on Methadone some addicts continue to use opiates for the high while using Methadone to avoid the withdrawal symptoms. Methadone has been used in the treatment of opiate addiction, but it is not the answer. Perhaps the government should be putting additional funding into opening more treatment facilities rather than more Methadone clinics. Good Luck Stephanie.

• • • •

TOO MUCH PARTYING

• • • •

DEAR BARB:

It's the New Year and I can't believe I did it again. I got drunk on New Year's Eve and made a fool of myself. I literally was dancing on a table, or so I was told! My date was a guy I have been dating for only a few weeks and we haven't spoken to each other since. I think he was embarrassed, as his parents were at the party and this was the first time I met them.

I don't know why I do these stupid things. Last year I did the same thing. I have good intentions, but I get partying and having a good time and just lose it. Do you think I have a problem that I need help with, or is it just a matter of controlling myself? Help! Christina

• • • •

HEY CHRISTINA:

Happy New Year! You said you did this last year too; do you only do this on New Year's, or does it occur at other celebrations? If it only happens at New Year's, I think it is a matter of controlling your intake of alcohol. For example, alternate your alcoholic beverages with pop or juice or best of all water. This way you can reduce your alcohol intake while still having something to drink for toasting or whatever. If you don't feel you can do this, it might be a good idea to choose not to partake in New Year's Eve celebrations.

These are some questions you can ask yourself: Are you drinking alone or in secrecy? Do you create excuses to justify drinking, such as to relax or manage stressful situations? Do you feel hung-over even when you haven't been drinking? Have you experienced blackouts or memory loss?

If you agree with any of these questions you could have a drinking problem and may want to seek professional help. Hope this information is helpful.

Part 3 - HEALTH - "Health is the greatest possession, contentment is the greatest treasure, confidence the greatest friend. Non-being is the greatest joy." - Lao Tzu

••••

HEALTHY WEIGHT LOSS

••••

DEAR BARB:

Hi, I read your column often and I was waiting for one to come out about struggles with dieting in the New Year. I am looking for a good diet since I need to lose about 40 pounds. It seems every time I hear about a great new diet, within a year it turns out to be unhealthy in one way or another. I was just getting ready to start the keto diet and yesterday I saw something on the news saying it wasn't a healthy choice for the long term. I have even tried to go vegan, but I ended up feeling unwell and my doctor thought I wasn't getting enough protein. It seemed to require so much work that I went back to eating meat.

I just want a way to eat so I can lose some weight, remain healthy, and be able to sustain it long-term. Is that even a possibility? - Candice

••••

HI CANDICE:

You have the first column of the year on dieting. What you are asking is a possibility. I agree the dieting industry is constantly changing and it's difficult to know if the diet you choose will be healthy and sustainable. Three of the top weight loss diets in 2019 are the Mediterranean Diet, WW (formerly Weight Watchers), and the Vegetarian Diet. Researching each of these diets will help you to find a way to eat to lose weight and stay healthy for the long term.

Three of the worst diets for weight loss in 2019 are the Carnivore Diet, the Whole30 Diet, and the Keto Diet. Do your research and find out. Also, consult the Canada Food Guide[5]. The Guide will provide you with information on maintaining a balanced and healthy diet and ways to develop healthy eating habits, such as eating mindfully. Don't eat on the run; sit down and pay attention to what and how you are eating; basically, enjoy your meal.

Diets that provide rapid weight loss are proven repeatedly to be temporary, and when the weight comes back, it is usually with a few extra pounds, thus resulting in the yo-yo effect. Staying active should also be included in a healthy weight loss program. Choose to walk rather than drive when possible. Include a yoga or meditation class as part of your daily routine. When feasible use whole food rather than processed. Take the time to prepare veggies and fruit for snacks rather than grabbing a bag of chips or sugary snacks. If fresh fruit is not available, choose unsweetened, frozen, or canned. Frozen veggies are a better choice than canned, as canned is usually high in salt. Stay hydrated by drinking lots of water rather than pop or other sugary drinks. Make sure to eat at least three meals

---

5. https://food-guide.canada.ca/en/

a day. When you make good food choices you will naturally lose weight, but give it time, if you want the weight to stay off you have to make a lifestyle change and stay with it. Diets offer short-term results that do not last. Thanks for your letter Candice.

• • • •

TOO MUCH ON MY PLATE

• • • •

DEAR BARB:

I am really stressed out and in need of some advice. I'm a single mom with two boys plus I work full time and attend university online. My mother was just diagnosed with stage four cancer. I am so filled with anxiety that I just don't know what to do. I can't seem to do it all anymore. Once I get the boys off to school all I want to do is crawl back in bed. I have a hard time sleeping through the night since my mind is constantly racing from one thought to the next. I'm short-tempered with my kids and feel awful about it. My boss is not too happy that I have to take time off work to take my mom for her chemo treatments. Since my dad passed away a few years ago, my mom is alone. I haven't had time to start the two courses I'm registered in so I may end up dropping out. I can't seem to prioritize anything.

Should I withdraw from my courses or take a leave of absence from work? I just don't know what to do. My ex takes my kids every other weekend, so I get a bit of a break. Sorry for my ramblings, but I just need some direction. - Thanks, Lynn.

• • • •

HI LYNN:

Thanks for sharing your story. I'm so sorry to hear about what you are going through. From what you are describing it seems you are most likely suffering from either anxiety depression, or a combination of both. Once you get in the grips of either of these conditions, they are very difficult to overcome without some intervention. As things start to build up, you become overwhelmed and often don't even realize it until you can't function any longer. Medication and some type of counseling, either on your own or with a support group, may help you work through this difficult time. A visit to your physician is the best place to begin, as they will be able to direct you to the proper facilities or prescribe the necessary medication. Understandably, you can't prioritize right now, your mind is spinning, and you need to get help to calm this first.

Be aware of some common symptoms of depression and anxiety. Depression – lack of interest in activities that you previously enjoyed, lack of energy, insomnia, trouble concentrating, increase or decrease in appetite. Anxiety – excessive worry, difficulty concentrating, sleep disorder, irritability, restlessness. As you can see, they overlap in some areas. A counselor would help diagnose the treatment that is best for you. Also here is an online test for depression or anxiety. https://depression.org.nz/is-it-depression-anxiety/self-test/. Best of luck Lynn.

....

UNIMAGINABLE DIAGNOSIS

• • • •

DEAR BARB:

I hate to bring up such a somber subject, but, in December, my husband was diagnosed with cancer of unknown origin. We were both devastated, but with the Christmas celebrations, we managed to put cancer out of our minds. Now that the holidays are over, we are faced with the unthinkable. My husband was given months to live, with the treatment he may have a year. We haven't told our family and friends yet. I don't know how I can live with this. I have had a couple of friends who lost their parents to cancer, but never a spouse.

I don't know how I can offer support to my husband when I can't manage myself. What is going to become of our relationship, and how will it change? I'm just wondering how people do this, maybe you or some of your readers have some suggestions to help me cope with this horrible situation. Thanks for any help you can offer. – Brenda

• • • •

HI BRENDA:

I am so sorry to hear about this diagnosis. Cancer is a terrible disease. So many of us have had to face this as we go through life, but there is always hope. A lot of progress has been made with cancer treatments and even living a few months longer than diagnosed can bring happiness to the patient and their loved ones. So, I would like to start by saying never give up, but also be realistic. If treatment is not helping and you are running out of options, you must accept the inevitable.

Fortunately, there are things you can do to make the time your husband has left as comfortable and fulfilling as possible. Try to focus on the present, not what may be in the future; the present is all you have, and, at this point, you need to cherish it. Enjoy the little things in life, like spending time watching a movie, or going for a walk. These things will become more important as your husband's health declines. You have to accept the situation as it is, you can't control the outcome, and acceptance will make this journey easier for both of you. As the disease progresses don't be afraid to ask for help.

There are resources your oncologist can recommend that will assist with the care you both require as your husband declines. Most likely you will begin the grieving process before your husband passes, and that's ok. Your emotions will flip-flop. One day you will be filled with hope and the next you will only see doom and gloom. Through it all hang on to hope, nothing is set in stone. Many people who are diagnosed with a terminal illness live for many years, but you have to maintain a balance between hope and reality. This is your new normal. Do your best to create memories. Maybe some readers will send in their thoughts and experiences. All the best to you and your husband,

••••

AGING GRACEFULLY

••••

DEAR BARB:

Hi, I am in my thirties and most of my friends are around my age or a little older. We are all starting to get crow's feet and sunspots on our skin. I am okay with this, but a lot of my friends are spending loads of money on Botox, filler, and other anti-aging procedures. When I'm around them I feel like I look so much older.

I don't want to spend my money and time on these procedures, but I hate being the old-looking one in the group. Any suggestions on how I can resolve this feeling within myself? Feeling old in Halifax! Thanks, Sharon.

• • • •

HI SHARON:

I can't believe you are feeling old and you're only in your thirties, although I can understand where these feelings are coming from. Many actors in the movies go to great lengths to look younger and that leaves the rest of us feeling much the same as you are feeling. What they are doing is superficial, you can't stop the clock. We are all aging, and these procedures only delay outward appearances, and it is an expensive regime to keep up. What would happen if they suddenly couldn't afford these procedures? Ultimately, the aging process would catch up with them and it would be a quick return to reality. You are accepting of yourself, and this is what most people strive to achieve.

My advice to you is to not compare yourself to anyone, it is not necessary. The other day I read an interesting quote by Theodore Roosevelt that would apply here: "Comparison is the thief of joy." Be happy with who you are and how you look.

Thanks for your interesting question, I'm sure a lot of people will be able to relate.

• • • •

GOING THROUGH THE MOTIONS

• • • •

DEAR BARB:

I am a forty-year-old mother of three and lately, I have been losing my zest for life. I have gained a few pounds that I can't seem to lose, my hair is going grey, my eyesight isn't as good as it used to be, and I know I'm going to have to wear glasses soon. I just feel like I'm falling apart physically and emotionally. My friends can't understand why I feel the way I do. I have a great husband, my kids are all healthy, and I have a job that I love, but I still feel that I'm missing something in life. My husband attends church regularly, and I used to go with him, but I just don't feel like going anymore.

Nothing seems to make me happy. Not sure what I can do to get out of this slump. Feeling sad, Dina.

• • • •

HI DINA:

My first reaction is to ask if you have discussed this with your family doctor. You need to make sure there is nothing physically going on with you. Many physical conditions can cause depression and feeling low. For example, a condition called hypothyroidism can mess with your metabolism and cause low energy, weight gain, and just an all-around sluggish feeling. Also, at forty years of age, you may be in perimenopause and that could cause many of the feelings you are describing. Both conditions can be treated with medication. Begin with your family doctor. Once physical causes are ruled out you may want to speak to a counselor or life coach.

Many women reach your age and start to burn out from spreading themselves too thin, with taking care of children, career, and household responsibilities. Perhaps you need to find your passion to bring back your zest for life. This could be anything, from learning to play a musical instrument, writing a memoir, or horseback riding lessons, the possibilities are endless. Remember, it's important to take care of Dina.

PART 4 - FRIENDS & NEIGHBORS - "What you do not want done to yourself, do not do to others." – CONFUCIUS

REVEALING NEIGHBORS

• • • •

DEAR BARB:

I have just moved into a new neighborhood, and I think I may have picked a questionable area. I have noticed two of my neighbors walking around their house naked. Another person does their gardening naked, mind you, they do have a five-foot fence around their yard. But from a certain angle, I can see right into their backyard. It seems odd to have two neighbors on the same street who do this. These neighbors are fairly friendly with each other and visit often. I have two children under the age of seven and I don't want them being exposed to this. Is there a law against doing yard work while naked? My husband doesn't see a problem with it, he says we should just ignore them and not look in their yard. Maybe I'm just a prude? What do you think? - Victoria

• • • •

HI VICTORIA:

Interesting neighborhood! According to the Government of Canada, the Criminal Code regarding nudity is as follows:

• • • •

NUDITY

Everyone who, without lawful excuse, is nude in a public place, or is nude and exposed to public view while on private property, whether or not the property is his own, is guilty of an offense punishable by summary conviction.

• • • •

IT SOUNDS TO ME LIKE your neighbors are committing an offense, so you do have the right to report them and hopefully, they will cover up. Some individuals feel these laws violate their freedom of expression. One man decided to go to a Tim Horton's buck naked[1] to order his morning coffee. Employees commented that the sight of his genitals made them uncomfortable. Brian Coldin of Bracebridge Ontario ended up serving five months of house arrest followed by twelve months probation. Other parts of the world, like the Netherlands and Spain, are more relaxed about nudity laws. Something to keep in mind is "World Naked Gardening Day" (WNGD) which falls on the first Saturday of May. I'm not sure why they chose that day, as in some areas it can be very cold. According to NBC News Today, WNGD "has become an annual tradition that celebrates weeding, planting flowers and trimming hedges in the buff." It is meant to be a light-hearted, fun day with no political implications. Here are some humorous do's and don'ts: https://youshouldgrow.com/world-naked-gardening-day/. I would not want my young children exposed to these neighbors either, so, no; I don't think you are a prude. Thanks for sharing your interesting dilemma.

---

1. https://www.thestar.com/news/canada/2012/01/12/ontario_man_found_guilty_in_nude_drivethru_incident.html

POLICING ALCOHOL USE

••••

DEAR BARB:

We have some friends that we hang out with occasionally and lately, I've noticed some tension between them. When we get together, we often go to an event and have some drinks. The last couple of times we went out I've noticed that Brig seems to be monitoring how much alcohol Cindy is consuming. When I ask Cindy if she would like a glass of wine, Brig answers for her and often says she will have just a little bit. Meanwhile, Cindy says sure I'll have a glass. I ignore Brig's comments, as I feel Cindy is an adult and she can answer for herself. I don't think Brig likes that and it is creating tension between us. As the evening progresses and Cindy drinks more it becomes obvious that Brig is annoyed with her. I must admit she does seem to be drinking more lately since she has experienced some traumatic events. However, I don't find Cindy confrontational or argumentative when she drinks, but more talkative and a little rougher around the edges than when she is not drinking. So, her personality does change a bit. My husband and I like them as a couple, but we don't like this tension developing between us. What is the right thing to do, should I do what Brig wants or what Cindy wants? - Confused Carla

••••

HEY CARLA:

You say your friend has gone through a difficult time, so perhaps this is just a temporary situation; however, alcohol is not a healthy way to cope. I don't think you should do what your friend's partner wants you to do, but you also have to be responsible. If your friend becomes belligerent is causing problems, or is attempting to drive, then you need to say no to the alcohol when they are at your home. I don't see any evidence of that in your letter. Possibly bad behavior on the part of Cindy begins when they leave your home and Brig is trying to prevent this before it begins.

You may want to go out for coffee with Cindy and discuss the situation as you don't want to have this discussion where alcohol is available. She may agree that she is drinking too much and that Brig is only being helpful. If that is the case, then you know what to do. If she says he is trying to be controlling and she doesn't appreciate it and doesn't feel there is an issue with alcohol, then you need to make a judgment call and decide what you want to do. Perhaps you could do some activities with them that don't involve alcohol, and then you can determine if there is a problem within the relationship. If the tension between them only occurs around alcohol, then there very well may be an alcohol problem. Ultimately the problem is with the other couple, and they have to work it out, so possibly step back from the relationship a bit and see what happens. Thanks for writing Carla.

• • • •

NEGATIVE NELLIE

• • • •

DEAR BARB:

What can I do about a friend who is so negative that she is driving me crazy? When we get together all she does is complain about her family, our friends, and her coworkers. If I try to point out something positive, she tells me I don't know the whole story. I'm starting to wonder why we are even friends. I don't know if I have changed, or she has. I have been trying to live a more positive lifestyle, so maybe I just didn't notice this about her before. I do not look forward to getting together with her.

Do you have any advice on how to best deal with a Negative Nellie? - Happy Hanna

• • • •

HI HANNA:

Negative people can be very difficult to spend time with. I guess you have to try to understand where the negativity is coming from. She may have learned it in her family, or she may have experienced a lot of negativities in her own life, which makes it hard to see the good in the world. Understanding where it comes from is not going to make it any easier for you to deal with. My suggestion may be to keep your visits brief. If she asks why you don't want to spend more time with her, be honest. Tell her how you feel; often people aren't aware of their personality issues but be prepared for her reaction.

It's very difficult for some people to confront their issues, so you may be putting your relationship in jeopardy. You could choose to counter her negative remarks with positive ones. Negativity can be a comfort zone for some people and in that case, change has to come from within. Great question!

• • • •

EXPOSING FRIENDS

••••

DEAR BARB:

My husband and I have been friends with another couple for the past five years. We have traveled together and often hang out on the weekends. A few weeks ago, we were all in our hot tub when Maureen took off her bathing suit top. I was totally shocked, but my husband seemed somewhat entertained by her actions, while Maureen's husband seemed to share my reaction. After a few awkward moments, Maureen put her top back on, and nothing was mentioned for the rest of the evening.

After they left, I talked to my husband who said "Oh, it was nothing, she was just playing around." But I was upset by it, and my husband and I ended up in a big fight. We haven't seen them since that night. I am concerned about whether we should continue to socialize with them. My husband thinks I'm overreacting. What do you think? I think if we added some alcohol or weed to the situation, things could get out of hand. - Shocked in B.C.

••••

DEAR SHOCKED:

I think your concerns are reasonable. Your friend probably was looking for a certain reaction, perhaps from the men. It might be a good idea to discuss this with her. It was an inappropriate thing to do, and I would be concerned about what she might do next. Your husband's reaction seemed a bit strange. How would he feel if you were the one taking your top off?

I would probably put a bit of distance in your relationship with this couple. Thanks for your letter.

• • • •

BATTLING JEALOUSY

• • • •

DEAR BARB:

Hi. I am having a problem with my best friend. We have been friends for years and things have always been pretty good between us, but recently our relationship has changed.

Mel had been dating a guy for about five years and she recently found out he was cheating on her. Her boyfriend ended the relationship and now he's with the other girl, who happens to be a mutual friend. Mel feels extremely betrayed and is angry at everyone, especially me. I have never seen this side of her; she disagrees with me about almost everything that we used to agree on.

She has done this with some of her other friends, but only the ones who have boyfriends. I'm wondering if she is jealous. Even if I talk about beliefs that I have, she will try to correct me and at times even say, "You are wrong!" We have been friends for so long and I hate for this to happen to us, but I don't know how to handle it. I have tried ignoring her comments, but then she almost challenges me to try to get me to react. She also does this on social media. If I share something I believe in, she will criticize it, again, trying to get me to react. Do you have any ideas on how I can deal with this, without losing a good friend? – Cynthia

• • • •

HI CYNTHIA:

Thanks for your letter. It almost seems as if two things are going on here. Your friend seems both jealous of the fact that you have a boyfriend and is trying to challenge your beliefs. This could be a form of baiting. Baiting is when someone deliberately attempts to get an angry or emotional reaction from another person. Your friend may be doing this intentionally, but it's more likely she is jealous that you have a boyfriend; especially since you say she does this to other friends who have boyfriends.

Your friend just experienced a devastating loss and betrayal by someone who I would assume she was in love with; so, you may want to try to be understanding. Take the initiative to open the lines of communication and find out what she's feeling. Be supportive and encouraging. Spend some time with her - just the two of you. Try not to react to her comments on social media but tell her in a private message how they make you feel. Don't feed into her anger. If this doesn't help, maybe take a bit of time away from each other.

Don't give up on the friendship but allow her some time to heal. I hope this helps. Good Luck Cynthia.

• • • •

PROPER TEXTING

• • • •

DEAR BARB:

I'm wondering about the rules of texting. I have some friends that I text, and they get back to me right away, but others take days. I personally feel it is rude for someone not to answer a text; it would be the same as not answering a voicemail or email.

Often text replies are made up of abbreviations and are difficult to interpret, like "u" instead of "you." I find this annoying, why can't someone take the time to answer in complete sentences? Another thing that bugs me is when I have a family gathering or friends for a BBQ and everybody is on their phones texting or checking emails. Really can't they wait until after dinner? The worst is when I am texting someone, not during dinner of course, but we get into a long conversation and, suddenly, they stop texting and I'm left hanging. I don't know whether I should send another text, or just assume the conversation is finished. If I send another text right away, I think I will appear desperate or needy.

Finally, is it okay to text another person while you are having a face-to-face conversation with someone? I do that sometimes, but only if I have to. If someone texts while I am trying to have a conversation with them, I am left feeling that our conversation is not very important to them. What do you think? Am I just overreacting and making a big deal out of this? Thanks, Cheryl.

• • • •

HI CHERYL:

Texting is a fairly new way of communicating, and, for people who are uncomfortable talking on the phone, it is a great way to keep in touch. However, some rules should be followed. Many situations depend on who you are with and how comfortable they are with you texting while in their company. Loosely followed texting etiquette rules can be found at Grammarly[2].

Here are some brief tips to follow. Do not text and drive, ever! It's always a good idea to send a text when you know you are going to be late for an event. Know when to call someone, as opposed to texting, as some things need to be said over the phone, or in person. Know when to put your phone away. For example, if you are visiting your parents or grandparents, leave the phone in your purse or pocket. If you are on a date and spending most of it on your phone, it may be a short-lived date.

Take time to write your texts and read them over before sending them. Always respond when someone sends you a text, even a one-word answer indicates the text has been received. Lastly, make sure you are texting the right person; there is nothing worse than sending a text to the wrong person. You may be overreacting Cheryl, but this is a new way of communication, and the kinks have to be worked out. Thanks for your letter.

••••

ROOMMATE IS A SLOB

••••

DEAR BARB:

I am a first-year university student, living on my own for the first time. My roommate is a friend that I grew up with and this is also his first time living away from home. I can't think of an easy way to say this, but my roommate is a slob!

---

2. https://www.grammarly.com/blog/texting-etiquette/

He leaves his clothes all over the house, dirty dishes are everywhere, and the bathroom sink is full of toothpaste and hair. I won't even try to describe the shower. We have a cat and he never cleans out the litter, even though he was the one that wanted the cat.

When I bring friends over, the smell from the litter box is overwhelming. I can't stand it, but I don't know how to approach him. He is a great guy otherwise and we get along terrific. I don't want to lose him as a roommate, but I don't know how much longer I can live like this. What should I do?
– Jim

• • • •

HI JIM:

Thanks for writing. I can relate while growing up my sister and I shared a room, and she was also a slob. Now, as adults, her house is immaculate and mine is less so. Go figure!

My first suggestion is to tell your roommate how you feel. Choose your words carefully, as you don't want to put him on the defensive.

You mention that your roommate is a great guy and that you get along well. Therefore, you should be able to sit down with him and work out a housekeeping schedule. Take turns cleaning. For example, every Monday you clean the bathroom, every Tuesday your roommate cleans the kitchen, etc.

Be specific; don't leave out any household chores. I assume you each have your own room. Keep in mind, if your roommate chooses not to keep his room tidy, there is not a lot you can do about it, since that is his personal space.

It may take a few weeks to get this schedule working effectively, especially if you have been doing all the cleaning up to this point. As your roommate begins to realize you are not going to do it, chances are he will. I'm not saying he will be happy about it, but hopefully, he will do it. He probably grew up in a family where someone else did all the cleaning and picking up after him. He will soon realize part of being on your own is cleaning up after yourself.

LEERY ABOUT ROOMMATE

DEAR BARB:

Hi, I am in my last year of high school and have been applying to universities and colleges. Last week I received my first acceptance letter from a top-notch university, and I will be living in residence at least for the first year. My dilemma is that I am a little leery about having a roommate. I am an only child and therefore always had my own room. I've heard all kinds of horror stories about bad roommates and I'm hoping I can avoid this happening to me.

Do you or your readers have any tips on how to get along with a roommate? I don't want to start off with problems. Thanks, Jay.

HEY JAY:

Congrats on being accepted at a first-class university, this is the first step on your life journey. Understandably, you would feel a little apprehensive about moving in with a total stranger. You could be meeting an awesome person who becomes a lifelong friend, or you could end up with someone you really can't stand.

The most important aspect of making this a successful union is communication. Communication is the cornerstone of any relationship. Once you are both unpacked and somewhat settled in, ask your roommate to join you for a coffee. Chat about what is important to you, share your schedules, and discuss whether you prefer to study in your shared room or the library. If you choose to study in the room you will need to have some undisturbed, quiet time. Discuss whether you will be having friends in your shared room and perhaps set times when your room will be friend-free and most importantly respect each other's privacy. It might be a good idea to let your roommate know ahead of time if you will be bringing friends home just so they are not caught in an uncomfortable situation. You will need to discuss keeping the room neat and tidy. Keep in mind that some people need more sleep than others, so be respectful of each other's schedules. It is also important that you respect each other's property, which means do not eat each other's food or borrow each other's clothes, (this would be more apt to happen with female roommates).

When, or if a conflict arises, discuss it right away. If you find confrontation uncomfortable, try texting your roommate with your concerns. This will start the conversation and then hopefully you will be able to discuss the situation face-to-face. There may be Residence Programs Assistants on campus with whom you will be able to discuss issues. Good luck Jay.

PART 5 - DATING - "To be fond of dancing was a certain step towards falling in love." - JANE AUSTEN

FRIENDS OR LOVERS

DEAR BARB:

My boyfriend and I have been dating for six months. He's an awesome guy, but I don't feel sexually attracted to him. We have lots in common and spend a lot of time together, but when it comes to intimacy, everything changes. Our relationship has been this way right from the beginning, but I kept hoping it would change. We can go weeks or even a month without any intimacy, or even kissing. We have never talked about it or acknowledged it in any way. We just ignore it, as if it isn't important. If he stays over at my place, we sleep in the same bed, but there is no hugging, we go right to sleep. When he leaves, he kisses me, but just a peck on the cheek.

I don't know how he feels about this, but it is beginning to wear on me, and I notice myself becoming attracted to other men. I am scared to bring this up because we may end up breaking up, and I enjoy his company. On the other hand, maybe I am just prolonging the inevitable. Looking for any advice you can offer. – Stephanie

HI STEPHANIE:

Thanks for your letter. As you know, sexual intimacy is an important part of any relationship, but what is more important is that you communicate how you feel. Sexual intimacy for some people is not a priority, and, if both parties feel the same way, there is no issue. However, when one party is not happy with the situation, problems can arise. Since you mentioned that your relationship has always been this way, it's interesting that you chose to stay. Usually, the strongest attraction is at the beginning of a relationship, and if it wasn't there at that time, it's unlikely to begin later. You may want to consider how long you are willing to stay in this relationship hoping it will change.

Perhaps you two are meant to have a friendship, rather than an intimate relationship. You can remain, friends, while you are in relationships with other people if this is what you both want. If you find it difficult to discuss this with your partner, you may want to see a counselor who may be able to help you discover if there are any underlying issues. For example, there may be medical reasons or emotional causes that are contributing. It's worth exploring further before you walk away. Best of luck in the future Stephanie.

• • • •

DIFFERENT WORLD VIEWS

• • • •

DEAR BARB:

My boyfriend and I have been dating for two years. We've always had a difficult relationship because we seem to see the world differently. For example, I am a saver, he is a spender. I am open and communicative, and he is a quiet brooder. I love kids; he's kind of so-so about them. I am very affectionate, but he isn't demonstrative at all. He smokes drugs quite often, while I don't use drugs at all.

Through all these issues we have managed to stay together, but now we are beginning to talk about marriage and I'm a little hesitant to commit. I don't want to spend my life fighting and arguing with my husband and I fear that would happen. I love my boyfriend and we have a lot of good times. I just don't know what to do. - Kim

• • • •

HEY KIM:

Partners who are very different can still have a successful marriage if they share similar core values. Some examples of core values include honesty, trust, commitment, and caring for others. You and your boyfriend should have a serious discussion about these issues and then you will be able to detect problem areas.

If the problem areas are concerning, I would suggest you go to couples' counseling before you commit to marriage. Your physician will be able to recommend a reputable counselor for you to see. Hope this helps Kim and thanks for writing.

• • • •

SEX AND LOVE

• • • •

DEAR BARB:

My boyfriend and I have been together for about five years. We love each other and get along great except for one thing, sex. When we first got together everything was great and we had sex pretty regularly. Over time it seems we are having sex less often. I am okay with that, but my boyfriend wants to do it more often. He has said he is afraid I'm falling out of love with him, but I'm not, I still love him tremendously.

How can I convince him I love him as much as always, but just don't want sex as often? – Jackie

••••

HI JACKIE:

Sex is a big issue in relationships and people are rarely on the same page all the time. Some people want more sex than their partner and some less. The main thing is to come to a mutual place where you can both be satisfied. Sometimes planning to be intimate on a certain night or afternoon will create some anticipation and increase your desire. For some people, spontaneity works better. This is something that you can work out together.

Sit down together discuss your desires and try to come up with a compromise, if you cannot do this then I would suggest you see a couple's counselor. Also, it is important to be attentive and affectionate towards your boyfriend, so he will still feel loved and appreciated. Thanks for your letter, Jackie.

••••

HOW OLD IS TOO OLD

••••

DEAR BARB:

I'm in my mid-thirties and have been divorced for quite a while. I share custody of my two children with my ex. I would like to have a partner to share my life with, but I'm finding it very difficult to meet men with whom I have anything in common. I'm a successful woman and find a lot of men my age are intimidated by my success, or compete with me.

A couple of months ago I met a man who is twelve years older than me. We have a great time together for the most part. Unfortunately, as time goes by, I'm finding a lot of differences between us that my friends are saying are because of our age difference. For example, he is not very demonstrative, which leaves me wondering where I stand with him. Also, he's talking about retirement, while I feel my career is just beginning. He has a son in college while my children are eight and ten years old. When he's around my children for long periods I can see him becoming agitated. I just don't know what to do. I enjoy his company, but I don't know if we have a future together. Looking forward to your input. – Christine

••••

HI CHRISTINE:

Thanks for your great question. Age can be a factor in many relationships but often people can adjust and work through these issues. Twelve years is not a tremendous amount of time. Remember Anna Nicole Smith, who was in her twenties when she married J. Howard Marshall, who was 89 and just happened to be a millionaire. That's an extreme situation, to say the least.

If you have found someone with whom you get along and have a good time, I would suggest you don't give up just because of age. As far as him not being demonstrative, men and women in their twenties can be that way too; it is a personality trait and not related to age. All relationships require some adjusting, more so as we become older and set in our ways.

Since you share custody of your children with their father, your partner will not have to be with them 24/7, so that shouldn't be a problem. As for him talking about retirement and you being in a different phase of your life that could become a problem, but it doesn't have to. If he wants a companion to travel with and you are not able to, you will have to work out a compromise. These are issues that are quite a ways down the road. A lot of things may change by then.

Enjoy the relationship and see where it takes you. If two people love each other enough they can overcome almost anything. Hope this helps.

• • • •

DOUBLE DIPPING

• • • •

DEAR BARB:
I have been reading your column for a while, hoping I would see my situation in one of the questions, but I haven't yet. I am in my early twenties and just finished my second year of university. This year my roommates were both guys. I was a little hesitant to

move in with them, but they both had girlfriends and at the time I had a boyfriend. Throughout the year all three of us ended up breaking off our relationships. As a result, we spent a lot of time at home or going out to bars and partying together.

The problem is that I have become intimately involved with both guys. I feel awful and I don't know how it happened. We have not talked about it, but I believe each guy has a suspicion that I may be involved with the other. Since the school year is over, I am now in the process of moving back home to work for the summer. Both guys have been pressuring me to renew our arrangement for the next school year. I don't want to move back in with them, as my ex-boyfriend has contacted me and there is a possibility we may reconcile. I don't want to tell my boyfriend about what happened with my roommates, but I fear it will come out since he knows both guys. I don't think my boyfriend would want to reconcile with me if he knew about what happened.

Not sure how to handle this situation. I know I messed up. – Dana

• • • •

HEY DANA:

You are right, you messed up! There are a lot of different things going on here. You say you don't know how this happened; you might want to spend some time trying to figure that out before you move into a relationship with anyone. Don't jump back into a relationship with your ex-boyfriend, as there were problems in that relationship that needed to be worked out, or you never would have broken up. Moving back in with your previous roommates you are just asking for trouble, as they may expect things to continue as before.

You must get away from this unhealthy situation and begin with a fresh start. At some point, when you have figured out exactly why this happened, and if you still want to reconcile with your ex-boyfriend, you need to discuss this situation with him. You don't want to enter a relationship keeping secrets from each other. Secrets always have a way of finding their way to the surface. Good Luck Dana.

• • • •

BOYFRIEND'S TWO-YEAR-OLD IS RUNNING THE SHOW

• • • •

DEAR BARB:

I have been dating this amazing guy for four months. We get along really well and rarely argue. We have a lot in common and I could see having a life with him, except for one thing, his two-year-old daughter! She lives with her mother but spends every other weekend with Brian. During the weekends when Katie is with Brian, I hardly see him at all. He doesn't seem to want to include me in his activities with his daughter. The few times I have met Katie she seems spoiled and wants to be the center of attention. I don't think this is right; I should be included in their activities. Am I way out of line? What do you think? - Sara

• • • •

HI SARA:

It's pretty typical for a two-year-old to want to be the center of attention, especially if she only sees her dad every other weekend. I think you need to back off and let your boyfriend decide when and how much involvement you will have in his daughter's life. The relationship is fairly new and perhaps he doesn't want his daughter to get attached until he is sure this relationship is going to last. I would say just let your boyfriend and his daughter have their weekends together, when the time is right, you will be included in these weekends. Great question Sara.

• • • •

UNFAITHFUL BOYFRIEND

• • • •

DEAR BARB:

My boyfriend and I have been dating for almost a year and I wasn't aware of any problems between us until recently. I just found out that my boyfriend slept with someone else. Last Saturday night he went to a party with some friends, while I went home to visit my parents for the weekend. One of my friends who was at the party told me my boyfriend got drunk and ended up having sex with a girl at the party. My friend didn't know who she was. I am devastated and don't know what to do. I haven't mentioned it to my boyfriend, and he hasn't said anything, although he has been acting pretty sheepish. Not sure if I should bring it up or wait for him to mention it. I'm not even sure I want to continue in this relationship. I don't think I will ever be able to trust him again. Looking for some direction. Thanks, Madison.

••••

HI MADISON.

Before you make any decisions you and your boyfriend need to have a serious discussion about what happened and why. At that point, you will be able to decide for yourself how you feel about your boyfriend's explanation. You have to decide if you believe this was a one-time event or if there is a good possibility it will happen again. If you are unable to let this, go and move on with your relationship it will never work. Every time you disagree this will be brought up and rehashed.

Perhaps before you make the final decision you may want to go for some couples counseling, it will be beneficial to you both. Best of luck Madison.

••••

DOUBTING DEBBIE

••••

DEAR BARB:

I've been involved with a woman for the past six months. We are both divorced and in our mid-thirties. We connected and got along fantastically at the beginning. I thought everything was going well until a few months ago when she seemed to become insecure and had doubts about whether our relationship could work.

It seems no matter how much I try to reassure her that everything is fine, she continues to have doubts. We have already broken up once but were able to reconcile. I love this woman very much, but I don't know how to handle her constant doubts. I don't want to end this relationship, but I'm not sure how to make things better. Hope you can help. – Ken

• • • •

HI KEN:

Thanks for writing. You have a challenging situation, but because you are hanging in there, I'm sure this can be worked out.

First, do you know anything about your girlfriend's past? Has she had some difficult relationships, maybe some betrayals that could be triggering these insecurities and doubts? You said you are both divorced. Do you know the details of her previous marriage? Perhaps her parents or other family members are divorced, thus causing her to lose faith in the longevity of relationships. You indicated that these insecurities have only arisen in the last few months. Perhaps as the relationship is becoming more serious, she is growing fearful that something may happen to cause it to end.

Many events can prompt insecurities in relationships. As well, something in your behavior could be triggering her doubts without you even realizing it. You mentioned that you are reassuring her, but her misgivings continue. Have you sat down together to discuss the nature of her doubts? Does she have fears about your ability to be loyal and faithful to her? You must discover the basis of the doubts in order to discuss and resolve them.

This task may be more than the two of you can handle. Since you love this woman and want this relationship to succeed, I would suggest you both see a professional counselor.

Many couples seek counseling before entering marriage, as it is better to find out early if you can resolve problems, before moving into a more permanent living arrangement or a marriage. Good luck, Ken. I hope I was helpful.

• • • •

GIRLFRIEND UNCOVERED

• • • •

DEAR BARB:

My girlfriend and I have been together for two years. We get along great and have a lot of fun together. I thought I wanted to spend my life with her, but I'm having second thoughts. We're in our late twenties and, I get that we both have a past, but I thought we had discussed anything that would impact our relationship.

Recently I discovered some disturbing details. My girlfriend and her friend had a falling out and as a result, the friend told me that my girlfriend had made adult movies in the past. I thought this friend was just angry and making it up, but I couldn't get it out of my head until finally I asked my girlfriend about it. At first, she tried to avoid answering but eventually admitted that she had made a few movies back when she was in university because she needed the money. I was devastated! She said she didn't tell me because she was embarrassed and felt awful that she had done these movies and she hoped I wouldn't find out. Now I have all these thoughts running through my head, like what if somebody I know, or in my family, sees these movies, or maybe they already have? And I wonder what else she has done that she hasn't told me about.

Don't you think this is a significant thing to keep secret from someone you have been in a relationship with for two years? I'm just not sure if I can move on from this. I would appreciate any input you can offer. – Eric

• • • •

HEY ERIC:

This is an unfortunate situation. Often people do stupid things when they are young and don't realize the consequences could last a lifetime. Eric, you are the only one who can decide whether you can live with the fact that your girlfriend did these movies and the possibility that someone you know may see them. Do you feel she is hiding other things from you? If you don't have trust, you really cannot have a successful relationship. Put yourself in her position and you can probably see why she wouldn't want to tell you, although I do think she should have.

Honesty is always the best policy. Ultimately you have to do what you feel is right and what you can live with. Thanks for your letter Eric.

• • • •

GUESS WHO'S ON A DATING SITE

• • • •

DEAR BARB:

I have a dilemma and I'm not sure what to do. A very good friend of mine separated from her husband about four years ago and she has been seeing someone for the last three years. Another friend of ours recently broke up with her boyfriend and she has been on a few dating sites. While online, she saw our friend's present boyfriend's profile. Needless to say, she was shocked and didn't know what to do. When she told me about it I thought maybe it was an old profile that he may have forgotten to take off, but I'm sure he would have gotten some hits, so it's hard to say he forgot about it.

We don't know if we should mention it, or just let it be. Help!
- Sabrina

• • • •

HI SABRINA:

It's hard to know the whole situation. Maybe he changed his email address; so, doesn't realize his profile is still online and active. If that were the case the administrators would not be able to contact him either. It's a tough position for you and your friend, but I think you must look for signs from your friend. Does she seem happy in her relationship? Unless she says something to you, about suspecting he is on a dating site, I would not say anything to her about this. If your friend was able to see his profile anyone would be able to see it, including his partner.

He doesn't seem to be trying to hide it, therefore just continue your relationship with them both until when, or if, something changes. Thanks for writing Sabrina.

• • • •

JEALOUSY OR INSECURITY

• • • •

DEAR BARB:

I know guys don't usually read advice columns, but I occasionally read yours. I would like your opinion on a situation I'm in right now. My girlfriend and I have been dating for one year and we have a lot of fun together when we are alone. As soon as we get together with other friends she becomes jealous and possessive. She accuses me of checking out the other girls and paying more attention to them than to her. For the first few months of our relationship, she wasn't like that, but now it's constant. At first, I was flattered and thought she cared for me. But now it has become ridiculous. Even when we are walking through the mall together, she accuses me of looking at other women. It's very frustrating because I am in love with her. It's almost easier not to associate with anyone, but I don't want to lose all my friends.

A couple of my buddies told me I was better off without her and that there must be something wrong with her. What do you think, why would someone be so jealous? I could understand if I gave her a reason to be jealous, but I don't. I'm committed to her. Thanks for your help. – Scott

• • • •

HEY SCOTT:

I little bit of jealousy in a relationship is normal and healthy, but this seems to be overboard and destructive. You were clear in saying that you were not providing a reason for your girlfriend to feel this way, so obviously it is an irrational reaction. Jealousy is a response to a person's insecurity, not necessarily the conduct of the other party. First, let's look at the reasons for jealousy. Jealousy erupts from a fear of loss and insecurity. Your girlfriend may have had some losses in her childhood that became aroused when she entered into a relationship with you. Most likely she fears losing you, but what she's doing may end up accomplishing exactly what she doesn't want. Also, if a person's needs aren't being met in a relationship, they may feel threatened and insecure.

There are things you can do to help to reduce your girlfriend's feelings of jealousy. Make her feel appreciated, loved, and important to you, which will help her to feel more secure within the relationship. Another thing you can do is tell her how her jealousy makes you feel. Perhaps she doesn't realize how you feel. Once you have done everything you can to reassure her, it's up to her to make changes within herself. If she is not able to do this, she may have to seek counseling, as this will only continue with her next relationship. You seem like a very caring boyfriend, best of luck in the future.

PART 6 - MARRIAGE & CHILDREN - "Being deeply loved by someone gives you strength, while loving someone deeply gives you courage."- LAO TZU

I WANT A DIVORCE

DEAR BARB:

I want a divorce, but my husband doesn't, and I don't know what to do! We have been married for seven years and have two beautiful children. I just don't feel the love for my husband any longer. We have been growing apart and rarely do anything together. We are almost like a divorced couple just cohabitating. Nothing happened to cause this; I just don't have any feelings for him. Well, I shouldn't say that, I do care about him, but only as the father of my children. Dan says he still loves me and wants to make our marriage work.

How can I convince him I want out of this marriage, and is there anything legally I can do? Needing advice. – Megan

HEY MEGAN:

My first question is, are you 100% sure this is what you want? Have you been to counseling alone or together? The decision to seek a divorce is one of the most life-changing decisions you can make and should not be made lightly. Are you sure you are ready for all that is involved in going through the divorce process—as it is difficult for everyone? There are several things you need to ask yourself, beginning with whether you still have feelings for your spouse, you say you don't love him, but you care about him. Are the problems you're experiencing a result of your relationship, or possibly financial, or work-related? There are people you can see to help discover what is causing this unhappiness. Therapists, counselors, and even mediators may be able to help you to make sure this is the right decision.

You may be feeling excited about a new start and be thinking about what it will be like with a new partner, but consider all your options carefully, as research has indicated that children are never happy about their parents divorcing. Children want their families intact and their parents to stay together. One of the consequences of divorce will be that most likely the custody of your children will be split 50/50. That means you will only see your children half the time. Plus, there will be people in their lives that you don't know and there is nothing you can do about it. Your ex will be making decisions for the children that you may or may not agree with. Eventually, you will both meet other people and that's another hurdle to cross, as your children may not accept a new person, or you may not like your ex's new partner. I don't mean to sound negative, but all these things need to be considered. I am not saying that you and your husband cannot work through these issues, as many people do, but you need to be prepared. However, if the situation is abusive, then you have no choice but to seek immediate intervention for the sake of safety. The place to begin is with a visit to your family physician who can refer you to a therapist or marriage counselor. Do not jump into anything, take your time Megan.

••••

VIEWING PORN

••••

DEAR BARB:

I have a charming sister-in-law and I respect her opinion. One day, my wife and I and my sister-in-law, and her husband were discussing different things, and the subject of porn came up. She is sixty years old, and I am seventy-seven. I thought she was a very liberal person, but when I told her I look at porn all the time, she was very surprised and told me I shouldn't be watching it.

Is there something wrong with watching porn? - Big Red

••••

DEAR BIG RED:

Great question! I'm not sure I would be able to get into all the issues surrounding pornography within this venue. You did not mention how your wife feels about you watching porn. Perhaps your wife has spoken to your sister-in-law about how she feels about you watching porn and that is why your sister-in-law said you should stop watching it. Many people have strong feelings about pornography because often young girls and boys and women with addiction problems become involved in pornography against their will. Often the men watching pornography choose not to see this reality but rather convince themselves that the women on the screen are enjoying what they are doing. For the most part, this is false. If these women were happy about what they were doing, why would they be hiding this from family members? I believe that given the opportunity most women would get out of porn.

Ultimately it is up to you and your moral compass whether you watch porno or not. Ask yourself how you would feel if your daughter or granddaughter were involved in pornography. Given a choice I don't think it's a profession most people would choose. Thanks for your question Red.

• • • •

COMFORT OR BOREDOM

• • • •

DEAR BARB:

My wife and I have been together for five years and I feel the passion has died. I still love her, but our relationship has become more comfortable than passionate. I try to be affectionate and considerate to her, but I just don't know how to get the passion back.

Do you have any suggestions? Thanks, Ken.

• • • •

HI KEN:

People in relationships often mistake comfort for boredom, although, this is not true. It is normal for a long-term relationship to become comfortable. The passion is still there you just must work a little harder to bring it to the surface. Take your wife out for a special dinner, maybe to a place you went to early in your relationship, which may trigger some happy memories. The simple addition of candles to the dinner table, with the lights turned down will change the whole mood. Write her a poem or a romantic letter. Make all the arrangements for a weekend getaway, by that I mean not only book the room but if you have pets, make sure they are taken care of, make reservations at a nearby restaurant for dinner, and perhaps have flowers delivered to the room.

If a getaway is above your budget, how about a gift of lingerie, it doesn't have to be expensive, it is the thought that is romantic. Comfort is a good thing if it is not indifference, as that would cause you to grow apart. Happy romancing Ken.

• • • •

NO KIDS FOR ME

• • • •

DEAR BARB:

My husband and I are in our mid-thirties; we began dating at university and dated for four years before getting married nine years ago. Our life is mostly great, and we both have careers we love. The problem is my husband now wants to start a family and I don't. I feel awful because we discussed this many times through the years and agreed that we would have children once our careers were established. I am happy with the way things are.

I haven't told my husband how I feel; I just keep putting him off. But I think he is starting to realize that I don't want children.

I love my husband and do not want my marriage to end, but I genuinely do not see children as a part of my life. I don't know what to do. I would appreciate any advice you could offer. Thanks, Sarah.

••••

HI SARAH:

You've got yourself into a predicament! You and your husband agreed to have children at a certain time and now this time has arrived, and you've changed your mind. Your husband may feel this is a deal breaker. You need to discuss this with him to see if not having children would be an option for him. Have you figured out why you don't want children? Is it a fear of pregnancy, leaving your career for a certain amount of time, or another reason? Is it that you do not want children at this point, or do you never want to have children?

Before you discuss this with your husband, try to find out the true reason why you don't want children. You may have to see a counselor to help figure out the answer to these questions, and perhaps a solution. Ultimately, this is a decision you must work out together, and honest, open communication is a good place to begin the conversation. Best of luck Sarah.

••••

THIRD TIME'S A CHARM

••••

DEAR BARB:

I am in my early forties and about to enter my third marriage. My wife-to-be has also been married twice before. We are not having a big celebration because we both feel a little awkward having to deal with all the comments about a third marriage. I know I messed up in my previous marriages, but I feel like this is the right thing to do.

I don't know how to deal with the comments from others. Do you have any advice? – Jason

• • • •

HEY JASON:

Congratulations on your upcoming marriage. Three marriages are a lot, but the important thing is if you have learned anything from your failed marriages. Often people who experience multiple marriages are people who always believe they are right. If you are a person who constantly thinks they are right and everybody else is wrong, you may not be ready to enter another marriage. It takes two to make a mistake and in failed marriages, both parties have equal ownership.

As far as entering this marriage, you are the only one who knows what you truly feel in your heart. If you honestly believe this is going to work and you are marrying for the right reasons, then you need to hold your head up and ignore the negative comments. I know it's a hard thing to do, but it's your life and you cannot live it according to anyone else's values. Good luck Jason.

• • • •

AVOIDING DIVORCE

••••

DEAR BARB:

I have recently become engaged and plan to marry next year. I love my fiancé very much and we get along well. Both of our parents are divorced, and we don't want this to happen to us. I know there are no guarantees, but we both want to try to do the right things.

We were wondering if you could suggest some tips to keep our marriage strong and healthy. Thanks so much. - Cheers. -Vicki in B.C.

••••

HEY VICKI:

Congratulations! Marriage takes a lot of work and dedication from both people for it to be successful. It is a good idea to focus on starting your marriage off on the right path. Sometimes people begin their marriage with unhealthy behavior patterns and by the time they realize it, the marriage has broken down.

I have found the following behaviors to be important in maintaining a happy, healthy married life.

Make your relationship a priority

Make your spouse feel special.

Be honest and truthful with each other.

Communicate your needs and desires openly.

Don't allow arguments to escalate to the point of abuse or threats to leave.

Maintain commitments and agreements that you make with each other.

Don't hold grudges. Resolve your differences and let any grudges go.

Avoid being critical of each other. Instead, offer suggestions to change unhealthy behaviors.

Listen to what your partner is saying. Try not to filter events through past hurts.

Be thoughtful (e.g., call your partner during the day just to say hi).

Leave a special note in a place only he or she will find.

Maintain unconditional love in your relationship.

Work towards making your intimate relationship mutually satisfying.

Do not let your work or outside activities become a threat to your relationship.

Enjoy each other and do fun things together.

Develop mutual interests and activities that you can do together.

Share equally in household and childcare responsibilities.

Go on a vacation every year, even if it's only camping.

Don't focus on ME, but instead focus on US.

Do not take each other for granted.

If you both decide you want your marriage to work and are committed to this end, I don't see how you cannot be successful. As stated by Frank Pittman, "The secret to having a good marriage is to understand that marriage must be total, it must be permanent, and it must be equal."

····

A TRUTHFUL HEART

• • • •

DEAR BARB:

I have a six-year-old daughter who was recently diagnosed with a heart condition. She was born with it but we did not realize it at the time. Now she needs to take daily medication. My husband and I have not told my daughter about her condition. My husband feels our daughter doesn't need to know. I believe if we keep this from her, we are not being honest, and we have always stressed to her that Mommy and Daddy will always tell the truth. So, I think telling her is the right thing to do.

Also, I believe it would be better for her to know her condition in case something happens when she is away from us, so she will be able to tell people that she has a heart condition. What is your opinion on this? Thanks, Stephanie.

• • • •

HI STEPHANIE:

Sorry to hear about your daughter, but with all the advances in medicine today people are living normal, full lives with heart conditions. It is best to discuss this with your daughter's cardiologist before you do anything. Ultimately the final decision is up to you. I found a Web Booklet that has information about childhood heart disease[1]. Plus there are several books about children with cardiac issues that would be helpful.

---

1. http://www.heart.org/HEARTORG/Conditions/CongenitalHeartDefects/CongenitalHeartDefectsToolsResources/Web-Booklet-If-Your-Child-Has-a-Congenital-Heart-Defect_UCM_316608_Article.jsp

I agree that a child should be made aware of their condition, however, you have to be careful not to scare them, which is why it is a good idea to discuss this with her cardiologist first. Children are adaptable and learn to live in many situations. As parents, we want to protect our children from uncomfortable circumstances, but reality is full of ups and downs.

I believe it's best to prepare your children for these types of obstacles. Thanks for your letter Stephanie, hope this information will be helpful.

· · · ·

PERMANENT CHANGES

· · · ·

DEAR BARB:

My 15-year-old daughter wants to get permanent makeup and asked me to sign for her. She says all her friends are getting their eyebrows done. I am thinking about it, but I need a second opinion.

What is your opinion on permanent makeup for a 15-year-old? Confused Mom in Edmonton.

· · · ·

HEY MOM:

If it was my 15-year-old I would not allow her to get permanent makeup. A 15-year-old wears her makeup a lot differently than an 18-year-old would, not to mention that styles and fads change constantly. One year, eyebrows are thick and heavy, and the next year they are thin and barely there. So as a mom, I think you need to think about this. Following is an excerpt I found online about tattooing laws in Alberta:

In Alberta, there is no legislation specifically stating an age of consent for tattooing. However, as getting a tattoo technically requires entering a contract, tattooing facilities may require that you be 18 years old to get a piercing without parental consent.

Both Health Canada and the Government of Alberta have issued guidelines for tattoo artists. For example, in Alberta, Health Standards suggest that even people over 18 need to demonstrate "informed consent" by providing a dated consent form. This form acknowledges that: they are undertaking the procedure of their own free will; are not under the influence of drugs or alcohol and are aware that the tattoo is permanent.

For more information, see: Alberta Health and Wellness > Health Standards and Guidelines for Tattooing (PDF – 12 p.)

• • • •

BOYS WILL BE BOYS

• • • •

DEAR BARB:

I have three young boys in public school. We live in a small community in Ontario Canada. Yesterday morning I received a phone call from the principal at my children's school because my sons had arrived at school at 8:50 am rather than 9:00 am. Ten minutes! I have had several clashes with this principal, and at first, I thought he had it out for me because I don't fit the conventional mold of a typical mom: I am a tattoo artist and understandably I have many tattoos. I don't have a problem with people looking at me, but I do have a problem with people judging me. But when I talked to other moms, I learned they also had received a call. I find this ridiculous. How are we supposed to be sure that our children arrive at school at exactly 9:00 am? My sons are like all boys and dawdle on the way to school, so I send them a little early, so they won't be late.

My kids play in the schoolyard when it is not school time, I believe the schoolyard is considered a public use area, as is a park, so why can't they be in the yard at 8:50. The school is not explaining why this is their policy. We are not sure what to do or who to speak to about this. Do you have any suggestions? Desperate Melinda.

• • • •

HI MELINDA:

Great question. This seems to be an overreaction unless it's an insurance issue. I think the key to this whole dilemma is for you to find out more about this policy who implemented it and what their justification is. Have you attempted to discuss this with the teacher, vice principal, or principal? If you have and nothing was resolved, then you may want to contact your school board and speak to a board official or the school superintendent.

If you have still not been able to receive a satisfactory understanding or resolution, then you may want to contact the Ontario Ombudsman at 1-800-263-1830 or email info@ombudsman.on.ca. The office of the Ombudsman is used as a last resort. As well, you can access their online complaint form from the following website: https://www.ombudsman.on.ca/About-Us/Who-We-Oversee/School-Boards.aspx. Good luck Melinda.

••••

PLAYDATES, NOT BABYSITTING SERVICE

••••

DEAR BARB:

My letter is more of a pet peeve than a question! I have a few friends who have young children and we have play dates at each other's homes with our three and four-year-olds. My son is three years old, and I have a few friends who bring their infants with them to the play dates. I can understand this as a babysitter is expensive. The problem is when they come to my house, they often hand me the baby to hold while they go and play with the older kids. Don't get me wrong, I love babies, but I don't want to hold someone else's baby for two hours while they play with my son!

So please mothers, when you are going for a play date, if possible, find a sitter for your baby, or take care of them yourself! Thanks for letting me vent. – Brenda

••••

HEY BRENDA:

Well said! The only thing I would add is that perhaps you could stipulate these guidelines when you are establishing the play dates. This will prevent any hurt feelings and perhaps feeling singled out; as the rules have been established and clearly stated right from the get-go. Enjoy!

••••

OUT-OF-CONTROL TEENAGER

••••

DEAR BARB:

Hi, I'm a single mother of a teenage daughter that I had when I was quite young. Her father did not want to be included in her life, but he has financially contributed to her care throughout the years. I have always heard people talk about how difficult teenagers are, but I was not prepared for this! My daughter is 15 and has been involved in drugs and alcohol, plus she is skipping school. Last week I got a call from the school asking me to come in. The guidance counselor told me Miranda rarely attends class and when she does, she is disruptive. She won't listen to me, and we end up arguing all the time. I don't think this is normal teenage behavior. I tried talking to her father, but he still is not interested in becoming a part of her life. He is remarried and has two young children.

I have to deal with this on my own and I don't know where to turn. Do you have any suggestions? Looking forward to your advice. Thanks, Patricia.

••••

HI PATRICIA:

Thanks for writing. Your situation rings true with many parents of teenagers, and it is especially difficult if you are a single parent. Unfortunately, your daughter's father has chosen not to be a part of his daughter's life, as some of your daughter's problems may be a result of her father's absence. She may feel there is something wrong with her to cause her father to abandon her, but that is a deeper issue that may require counseling. It is normal for a teen to pull away from their parents and become more involved with their friends. They want to fit in and what their parents think is not important anymore, but children still need their parent's love and guidance. You must determine whether this is normal teen behavior or showing signs of a troubled teen.

Indications of a troubled teen may include a sudden change in appearance, involvement in a new peer group, totally disregarding rules that you set, and excessive abuse of drugs or alcohol. From your letter, it seems your daughter may have gone beyond normal teenage behavior, as she is not attending school regularly and seems to want to live her life according to her agenda, rather than what society requires. There may be several reasons for this change in your daughter's behavior, including depression. Some of the signs of teenage depression include trouble at school, running away from home, irresponsible behavior, and violence. It appears that your daughter is experiencing some of these issues.

My suggestion would be to go to your family doctor to see if you and your daughter can be referred to a family counselor. This is the first step in working toward a positive outcome—before things get out of hand. While going through this stressful time try your best to take time for yourself and relax and know that you will work through this. Many parents experience similar situations with their teenagers and ultimately end up with healthy happy adult children.

PART 7 - WORK - "Choose a job you love and you will never have to work a day in your life." – CONFUCIUS

COMING TO WORK SICK

DEAR BARB:

I work in an office with 15 other people. We get along well for the most part. My issue is people coming to work when they are sick. Why would someone do that and end up making everyone else sick? Two weeks ago, our receptionist came in coughing and sneezing, so she not only risked getting all of her coworkers sick, but she also put our customers at risk. As a result, four people in our office came down with a cold this week; obviously, they caught it from our receptionist. I understand that people may need the money and not want to lose pay, but we have six paid sick days a year, so why not take a few days off and get well?

I don't know whether I should bring this topic up at a staff meeting, or just accept that this is the way it is. Thanks, Marilyn.

HI MARILYN:

Thanks for your letter. I can completely sympathize with you. When people come into work sick and risk getting others sick it appears to be a selfish act on their part, however, there are several reasons why someone would arrive at work with an obvious cold or another ailment. The number one reason would be money. Even though you say you have paid sick days, often people want to save their sick days just in case a more serious illness occurs. Additional reasons may be that they fear missing an important meeting, or deadline and perhaps end up losing their jobs or being reprimanded.

Going to work when you are ill, is not good, whether it is a cold or an injury, as it may cause the illness to linger because you are not getting the proper rest required to recuperate. Making others in the office ill may cause a major reduction in overall production. According to a 2011 research study, sick days are costing the Canadian economy $16.6 billion a year, with the average worker taking 9.3 sick days. Mental health issues, possibly as a result of workplace stress, account for many of these sick days. I think it would be a good idea for you to bring this topic up at your next staff meeting, and, if you don't want to be seen as a problem, maybe you could discuss it with your boss before the meeting and have him bring it up.

Your boss would be more effective at encouraging employees to stay home when they are ill, by reassuring them that their job is not in jeopardy if they don't come to work when they are ill. Also, as a group, you may want to look into negotiating more sick days or see if vacation days can be used instead. Hope this information was helpful.

• • • •

STEALING FROM WORK

• • • •

DEAR BARB:

I work part-time in an office and a good friend of mine also works there. We have been friends for 10 years and get along great. We applied for jobs at the same place, and we were so surprised that we both got in. I am a mother of two young children and a part-time student. Kara has no children but is also a student. We are both struggling financially. Recently I noticed that Kara is taking a lot of supplies home from the office. At first, I thought it was just the odd thing and maybe some paper, or pens, but it seems to be escalating. For example, last week she took home, three reams of printer paper and an entire box of file folders, and that's only what I saw. She may have taken more items. When I mentioned something about it, she said, "They don't need it, they've got lots of money." The worst part is that she is selling these items online, which I just happened to see while browsing Facebook marketplace. The business that we work for is a small local shop and the owners work in the shop. I feel like I am between and rock and a hard place. I don't want to lose my friendship, but I don't feel what she is doing is right. I need some advice! Thanks, Danielle.

• • • •

HEY DANIELLE:

You are in a difficult spot. Should you do what is morally right and risk losing your longstanding friendship, or do you ignore what your friend is doing and perhaps try to encourage her to stop? Without a doubt, she will eventually get caught, and likely, the owners will charge her with theft, as obviously, she is stealing enough items to warrant her selling them online. She may end up in a lot of trouble, possibly even going to jail.

On the other hand, if she were to stop now before the missing items make too big of a dent in inventory, she may be able to move forward and maintain her job without being discovered. If she continues stealing and you don't come forward, there is a good possibility that because of your close relationship, the owners will assume you knew what was going on, or maybe even participated in helping your friend to steal these items, thus putting your job in jeopardy.

I think your only option is to advise your friend to stop, and if she doesn't, you are going to have to talk to the owners. The choice is yours. Thank you for writing Danielle and I believe you will do the right thing.

• • • •

PAINS OF GROWING UP

• • • •

DEAR BARB:

My sixteen-year-old son has been working as a host at a popular roadhouse for the last few months. This is his first job and he's doing well and getting lots of shifts. Recently my son went in for his shift and too many hosts had been scheduled to work and someone had to go home. One of the other hosts was a twenty-year-old girl with a child and she had not been getting many shifts. She made my son feel bad as she told him she needed the money, therefore he offered to go home so she could stay, even though he didn't want to.

As my son was leaving his boss pulled him aside and said he had tried to call the other host to tell her not to come in but couldn't get a hold of her. Clearly, this indicates they would have preferred my son stay. Since my son is so young, he gave in to the other hostess even though he would have preferred to work. Not sure how he should handle this situation if it comes up again. – Melanie

• • • •

HI MELANIE:

Your son has a good heart, but he needs to learn that the work world functions a bit differently than everyday life. Without a doubt, I believe this hostess was taking advantage of your son. She probably feels that since he is young and living at home and she has a child she needs the work more than him. If this situation arises again your son needs to let the boss decide who will go home. If no one volunteers he will have to make a decision based on seniority or whatever criteria they use. This is a good lesson for your son to learn if he is going to survive in the world of work. Cheers Melanie.

• • • •

TRICKY BUSINESS

• • • •

DEAR BARB:

I am in my fourth year of university and have been struggling to pay for my education. I work part-time as a waitress in a local pub, plus part-time in a bakery and I still have a hard time making ends meet. All my free time is spent studying, so I don't have a life. I've been reading the recent articles in The Voice

"Tricks for Tuition" and the subsequent editorial comments. I had no idea there was such a demand for this type of work.

I am seriously considering doing this for a while. It would certainly make my life easier. It can't be all that bad if 100,000 students have registered. What do you think? – Misty

• • • •

DEAR MISTY:

There are a lot of risks to this type of work, as stated in the articles. I don't think this is the type of work you can casually enter. You have to ask yourself if you are willing to compromise your morals and values without impacting your self-worth as a person. For some people, this isn't an issue. Is this a job you can share with people in your life, or would it be something you would keep secret? What about a future employer discovering that you were a sex worker? With social media, this may be difficult to hide.

I would suggest you continue with your current situation, as you have managed to get through four years of university, no doubt it has been difficult. Ultimately, it is your decision, but this is not something you should rush into. Good Luck Misty.

PART 8 - ETIQUETTE - "There is nothing more frightful than ignorance in action." - JOHANN WOLFGANG VON GOETHE

SURPRISE INVITATION

DEAR BARB:

Happy New Year Barb! I have a dilemma, a family member I rarely see is getting married this summer and I received an invitation to the wedding. I was surprised to receive this since we rarely see each other or communicate. My wife and I don't want to attend, but on the other hand, we don't want to cause problems or offend anyone.

What is the right thing to do? - Brian

HEY BRIAN:

There is no right or wrong in this situation. Do what feels right for you. If you decide not to attend, it would be nice to include a note with the RSVP, perhaps wishing them the best. On the other hand, maybe the intention of the invite is to break the ice and initiate some communication. So, ultimately, it is up to you.

Happy New Year to you as well.

DINNER ETIQUETTE

DEAR BARB:

A few nights ago, I was out for a birthday party; there were 12 of us at the table. My question is, "Should we wait until everyone is served before we begin eating?" It seemed a long time to wait until everyone was served, as our meals were getting cold. This doesn't seem right to me, what do you think? Thanks, Josh.

Hey Josh:

Good question. The general rule is if fewer than eight people are dining at the table, it is polite to wait until all are served. If there are more than eight people, usually it is acceptable to begin eating after three or four people are served, or your host may suggest you begin when you are served. Enjoy!

SENDING BACK AN INFERIOR MEAL

DEAR BARB:

My wife and I went out for dinner last Saturday night. We went to a restaurant that we had been to many times and the food was always great, but not this time. I ordered liver and onions and was very disappointed. The liver was gristly and tough, and the bacon was barely cooked. I wanted to send it back, but my wife didn't want me to. She didn't want me to because she was fearful the cook would be angry and do something rude such as spitting in my food.

I didn't agree with her and decided to complain to the waitress. She was very accommodating and told me they would take it off the bill and asked if I wanted a different meal. I chose not to order something else because my wife was angry, and she had put the thought in my head that the cook may spit in my meal. I wasn't sure what I should have done in that situation. What is your opinion? James

• • • •

HEY JAMES:

I agree with you. If you order a meal at a restaurant, you should be able to get the best meal available. If it had been me, I also would have sent it back and ordered something else. Whether the cook or server would spit in your meal is debatable. If you treat your server with respect and explain why you don't feel the meal is what you ordered, chances are there will be no problem.

In a decent restaurant, I believe the owner/manager will do their best to avoid hiring immature, resentful people who would stoop to the level of spitting in someone's meal. Becoming a chef is a very prestigious profession and I believe a good chef takes pride in the dishes they prepare. Good question James.

• • • •

ONE FRIEND TOO MANY

• • • •

DEAR BARB:

Hi! Every year around this time, a couple of girlfriends get together, and take our children for a bowling day. Last week I put a post on Facebook about the date and time and tagged my other two girlfriends. Another friend noticed the post and replied that she would be joining us. No one wants her to come, but we don't want to hurt her feelings either.

What is the best way to handle this situation? Thanks, Tamara.

• • • •

HEY TAMARA:

There is only one thing you can do. Be honest with your friend. Tell her this is a yearly event that you and these other friends do together with your children and that you hope she is not offended. Then leave it at that. Thanks for your letter and I hope this was helpful.

• • • •

NO KIDS ALLOWED

• • • •

DEAR BARB:

My husband is turning 40 and I would like to have a surprise party for him. I want to invite our friends, but I don't want any *kids at the party. I don't want to offend anyone; therefore, I'm not sure how to communicate this to my guests. Should I write it on the email invite, or would it be more personal to call everyone? Help! – Julie*

••••

DEAR JULIE:

It is impossible to go through life without offending someone. Understandably you would not want a houseful of children, as it is an adult party. My suggestion would be to add a note to your email invitation similar to the following: "This is an adult party, and your children would probably be more comfy at home in their own beds, rather than hanging around with a group of grownups. Looking forward to sharing this celebration with you."

Be prepared, as some people may be offended by their children not being invited, but you can't please everyone. Enjoy! Happy Birthday.

••••

TO BE TRUTHFUL OR NOT

••••

DEAR BARB:

Hi, I have a good friend whose brother opened a new restaurant. A bunch of us went there one evening for dinner and we didn't like it. The service was slow, and the food was not good at all. I know Carol is going to ask me what I thought, and I don't know what to say to her. Most of my friends didn't like it and said they would never go back.

Should I be honest with her and risk ruining our friendship, or should I lie and say I loved it? Carol and I have been friends since high school, and I would not want to lose her as a friend. Looking for some direction. Thanks, Jodi.

• • • •

HI JODI:

Great question, but not an easy answer. I don't think you should come right out and say you hated it, nor should you lie and say you loved it. Perhaps you could find something positive to say about the restaurant, for example, the decor is great, or the menu offers quite a variety, or the prices are good. This way you are sidestepping saying the food and service were bad. If the food and service are bad, it will come out and at least you will not have been the one to say it. Difficult situation.

• • • •

RENTING FAMILY COTTAGE

• • • •

DEAR BARB:

One of our relatives owns a cottage and family members use it for their vacations. We went there a couple of weeks ago and we were assured that we could have it to ourselves for the week; however, that was not the case. The owners of the cottage and their children arrived halfway through the week, so we all had to double up the sleeping arrangements so there would be enough room for everyone. Don't get me wrong, we love them, but we just wanted a week of peace and quiet. I don't think they should have shown up unannounced during the week we were using the cottage. A few family members think I am being unreasonable since the owners are letting us use the cottage free of charge and they feel they should be able to come to their own cottage. What do you think? - Lauren.

• • • •

HEY LAUREN:

I tend to agree with you. If the owners assured, you that you could have the cottage to yourself for a week then they should have kept their word. Maybe next time, you could offer to pay for your week. This may cause them to think twice before arriving since you are renting the cottage for the week. Thanks for the great question.

• • • •

STEALING SWEET DELIGHTS

• • • •

DEAR BARB:

I have a family member who visits occasionally and often stays overnight. I have noticed that, when she leaves, some of my baked goods are missing and I am pretty sure she is the one taking them. I love to bake and often have lots of homemade cookies and desserts to offer when people visit. This particular family member raves about my baking. I find it strange that she would steal from me when I would be perfectly willing to give her some to take home if she asked. It seems like such a sneaky thing to do.

What would be the best way to handle this without hurting her feelings or embarrassing her? Thanks, Rose.

• • • •

HI ROSE:

Thanks for your question. I agree with you that it is a bit of an odd thing to do. She doesn't want to ask you if she can take some baked goods home, however, she must realize that you know she is taking these items.

Next time she comes for a visit, early in the visit casually mention that you are going to prepare a package of goodies for her to take home. By saying this you are not putting her in a confrontational situation and nothing more needs to be said about it, as long as you remember to prepare her take-home goodies.

• • • •

PASSING GAS

• • • •

DEAR BARB:

Hi, I hate to bring this up, but my husband needs to learn something about social etiquette. I don't mean just manners; I mean passing air and burping! When we were dating, he had excellent manners, except for the occasional passing of air, which was understandable. Now he doesn't care where he is or who is around, if he has to break wind, he does. They are not the silent ones either. It is so embarrassing, but not to him. When he is around his family, they all laugh, it's just something they do. We have two sons, and I can already see it happening with them.

If I try to talk to my husband about it, he says I'm just overreacting, and that farting and burping are a normal part of life, so I need to get over it. Doesn't anybody have manners anymore? What do you think? Am I overreacting? - Tina

• • • •

HEY TINA:

Interesting topic, pretty sure this is a first for this column. Flatulence and burping are a normal part of everyday life and must be released. Research says that most people fart between 14 and 23 times a day. It may seem like a lot, but some just slip out and you may not even realize it. Farts are swallowed air that is introduced into your digestive tract through eating and drinking. Most are odorless, but depending on what you eat, they can have a foul smell. For example, animal proteins like meat and eggs produce more smelly farts than fruits and vegetables. There are things your husband can do to reduce the amount of gas he produces, although I'm not sure that is a concern for him. I will include ways to reduce gas and you can pass this column along to him. You never know, he may make some changes. Chewing gum will increase the amount of gas in your system, as you are swallowing more air. Eating slowly and taking the time to chew your food will reduce the amount of gas in your digestive tract. Be aware of gas-producing food and drinks such as beans, broccoli, whole grains, carbonated drinks, milk cheese, ice cream, and fruit. Unfortunately, these are all foods that are necessary for a healthy diet.

As to etiquette, did you know in some cultures (such as the Inuit of Canada) farting after a meal is interpreted as gratitude for a great meal? This isn't common throughout all cultures, though. I agree that passing gas of any kind should not be done in social settings. In your own home, I think that's a personal choice with whom you choose to share your farts. So, I do not think you are overreacting.

PART 9 - PANDEMIC - "There is nothing like staying home for real comfort." - JANE AUSTEN

• • • •

NEW RELATIONSHIP DURING PANDEMIC

• • • •

DEAR BARB:
As a result of being in isolation for so long, I believe we are probably learning something about ourselves and our relationships. The people I thought I would hear from I don't, yet other people who rarely contacted me before the virus are checking in and making sure I am okay.

Two months before self-isolation I began seeing a great guy. It was a relationship that I thought had a future, but now I'm starting to wonder. He contacts me daily through video and text messaging but I'm finding that I am not looking forward to hearing from him. I am thinking of ending the relationship. On the other hand, maybe it is just the situation. We didn't have a lot to talk about because we didn't know each other that well. Would that be cruel to end the relationship now in the middle of this pandemic, I know it is not cool to end a relationship through a text message, but this is different, isn't it? Looking for a second opinion. Thanks, Adrianna.

• • • •

HEY ADRIANNA:

Great question. These are unchartered territories, so I can only offer a guess at what would be ethical. Since you just met him, I think you should give it some more time. Of course, you don't have much to talk about because you are not doing anything; day in and day out is pretty well the same. You could take this time to learn about each other's growing up years and families. Following is a great site to help get to know someone. Included are 21 questions to ask a guy[1].

These are questions that would help you get to know each other and will undoubtedly lead to deeper conversations. I'm sure he is having similar concerns about what to talk to you about. Also, you don't need to talk all the time, as I'm sure you know there are games you can play with each other and friends, either online or by setting up a good web camera (like charades).

You will have to find a new way to relate. We don't know how long this isolation will last, but, as we've all been told it is necessary to stop this virus. My advice would be to try some of the above suggestions and see if you still feel the same. I would not suggest ending the relationship right now if you feel there may be a future. Take this time to relax and get to know each other, then see what the future brings after this virus is over. Thanks, Adrianna, for taking the time to write.

••••

PANDEMIC CRAZINESS

••••

---

1. https://dating.lovetoknow.com/21_Questions_to_Ask_a_Guy

DEAR BARB:

Hi, I am going crazy! I have been self-isolating for weeks. I am a single person and normally I like my own company, but this is getting to be too much. I am doing everything I can to keep busy; I work in a clothing store so I can't work from home. I have read all the books on my list, watched all the Netflix I had intended to, finished my puzzle and now what do I do? I go for walks numerous times a day. I used to take my dog with me but now when I ask if she wants to go for a walk she runs away and hides, so I go by myself. Some mornings when I wake up my feet are aching. I used to wonder why, I figured it out and it's all the walking. I talk to my family and friends as much as I can, but since none of us are doing anything, there is nothing to talk about.

My stress level is escalating. I know you are probably in the same boat as the rest of us, but maybe you would be able to offer some suggestions on how we can keep our sanity throughout this pandemic? - Crazy Carly.

• • • •

HI CARLY:

Thanks for your letter. Yes, we are all in the same situation if we are doing what we are supposed to be doing. It is difficult to be isolated and even more difficult if you are alone. If you are with your family, at least you have someone to talk to or get on your nerves at times. Carly, you seem to have done everything within the first few weeks and now you need to pace yourself, which means creating a daily schedule of things you want to accomplish. This will give your life some routine and something to look forward to. Walking is a good physical activity and will relieve some of the stress, but you need to set up certain times to walk. For example, go for a walk each morning and evening, and maybe only take your dog on one of these walks. It is extremely important to stay in touch with family and friends. Even if you touch base every few days, just to make sure everyone is coping. If you have a vehicle and can get out shopping, offer to pick up a few things for neighbors or family who are not able to get out. Leave the items outside their door and have them etransfer the money to you.

It's also very important that you do not spend a lot of time watching the news. You need to keep up to date but don't bombard yourself with negative information. Try to watch the news in the morning and the evening, which will be enough to keep you updated on any new developments. We all must remember this is temporary and will end and we will get our lives back. So, Carly, stay positive and be kind to others.

• • • •

VIRAL THEORIES

• • • •

DEAR BARB:

After weeks of isolation and hearing lots of stories about the coronavirus, I just don't know what to believe about how or when this virus began or how it will end. Everybody seems to have a different theory and they all believe they are right. The most common theory I have heard and read about is that Coronavirus is caused by 5G Internet. This theory originated when a woman created a YouTube video where she claimed that high frequencies from the 5G technology release chemicals that are inside of your body from the use of vaccines and chemicals in foods etc. and ultimately leads to symptoms like those of Covid-19. Another theory I read about is that the virus was created in a lab and released to the public.

And the one that most of my friends believe is that it comes from eating bats, apparently, someone in a market in China was eating soup that contained bat meat and that was the beginning of the virus. They all seem a little weird to me. I am choosing to self-isolate because it seems to make the most sense, plus there is nowhere to go anyway since everything is shut down. Maybe I am just thinking too much, but I wish someone could offer some insight or truth as to what is going on. Any suggestions on how to find some peace in this chaotic situation? Thanks, Mackenzie.

• • • •

HEY MACKENZIE:

Great letter. Many theories are circulating about where the virus came from and the one that seems to come closest to any type of validity is the bat theory. Scientists have discovered a similar virus to the covid-19 in bat DNA. The question remains, how was it passed from bat to human, as eating bat meat would not transfer the virus? Whether there was an intermediate host will be something for the scientists to figure out; our job is to prevent the spread.

As for the other theories you mentioned they have all been debunked. USA Today published an article on March 21 explaining why the 5G theory has no validity [2] and is well worth the read. As far as the claim about the virus being created by

---

2. https://www.usatoday.com/story/tech/columnist/2020/03/21/did-5-g-cause-coronavirus-covid-19-pandemic/2873731001/

scientists in a lab in India, and that the findings were circulated through social media, this has been examined by several scientists who study viruses and found to be unproven. Depending on your belief system many people have decided to accept one of these theories as truth. My suggestion is to follow the advice provided by professionals and health care officials, who have much more knowledge than we do about this topic. This seems to be working to a certain degree as a large number of Canadians have followed the advice to self-isolate, and the cases are not escalating as rapidly as they are in the U.S. President Trump was slow to get his people on the bandwagon, and the numbers show the difference. You can only continue doing what you are doing while keeping in mind that this will end one day, and we will go back to living our lives. Thanks for your letter and stay healthy Mackenzie.

• • • •

TOUGH TIMES

• • • •

DEAR BARB:

Hi, because of the coronavirus, my husband and I have been off work and home with our kids for weeks and we are stressed out. I know it's the right thing to do, but, oh my god, I don't know how stay-at-home parents do it. I have a 7 and 8-year-old and they are constantly fighting, and I am usually the referee. My husband seems to be finding stuff to do in the garage, so I am left with the kids. I am attempting to keep up their reading and math skills as their teacher sent work home for them to work on.

I know why I didn't become a teacher! I can't even send them to their grandparents, as that is too risky since my mom has a heart condition. I am also expected to do my own work from home, I am an accountant, so it's looking like I will have to do this after the kids go to bed since I have to concentrate.

I need some words of encouragement to get through this, as no one seems to know how long it will go on. Do you have any suggestions to make this time flow easier for our family and probably many other families? – Sandra

• • • •

HI SANDRA:

It's not an easy transition for families, but we have no choice unless we want what happened in China, Italy, and Spain to happen in Canada. The best thing for you, your husband, and your children to do is to make a schedule. For example, every morning the kids do their schoolwork and you will have to be available for them; therefore you don't want to get involved in your work, as you will be constantly interrupted. The Government of Ontario has a website offering educational sites[3] for parents and children.

Afterward, you could all go for a morning hike or some snowshoeing to burn off excess energy before lunch. Your husband could spend the morning on his work, while the kids are your responsibility. That should bring you to lunchtime. After a family lunch, you could spend some time working, but make it clear to your children that you are not to be disturbed. So perhaps this could be their time to watch a movie or play video games, or dad could take them out for a hockey or

---

3. https://www.ontario.ca/page/learn-at-home

basketball game—in the driveway, as parks are no longer a safe place to be—of course, this depends on the weather. This is just an example of a schedule you could implement; following a routine will help everyone get through this time of self-isolation. Kids do better when they have a schedule to follow. Many websites offer activities and games for children. This is one for children under 10 which you may find useful. https://www.commonsensemedia.org/website-lists.

Hopefully, we will all find our way through this and be able to look forward to an enjoyable summer.

PART 10 - LOSS - "Those who die without being forgotten get longevity." - LAO TZU

••••

DEVASTATING SIBLING LOSS

••••

DEAR BARB:

Recently I lost my younger brother to cancer. He was only thirty years old and just beginning his life. It was the worst experience of my life. He suffered for three years, and we all hoped he would beat this terrible disease, but, in the end, he succumbed. We're trying our best as a family to get on with life, but it's so hard. Every day I think about my brother and our childhood and all that he will miss. Sometimes I think about the times I was mean to him and feel so awful, I just want one more day with him to apologize and make things right. He was such a gentle soul, and always watched out for me. I feel so alone without him by my side.

Nothing in my life ever prepared me for losing my brother at such a young age. It just never crossed my mind that I would lose Steve, he was my heart. My whole family is devastated. How do we make sense of such a tragedy? Feeling sad in Calgary. – Melinda

••••

HI MELINDA:

So sorry for your loss. Losing a sibling is devastating at any age. When a parent loses a child everyone rallies around and supports them, however, often a sibling's grief is overlooked, and they are left to deal with the loss on their own. Whether you and your sibling were close does not make a difference, the loss is real and lifelong. We all have complicated relationships with our siblings, some are loving and caring, and others are fraught with jealousy and sibling rivalry. Your role in the family may affect your relationship with your siblings. Older siblings tend to be looked up to and idolized, while younger ones are often teased and not taken seriously and seen as stealing all the attention. No matter the relationship, there are things you can do to learn to live with and manage your grief. Most importantly, forgive yourself for things you may have said or done in the past; these things are all a normal part of the sibling relationship. Also, don't isolate yourself. Share your grief with your parents and other siblings and offer support to each other. Every person's pain is unique and real to them. Give yourself time to heal.

If you feel you are stuck and not able to move on with your life, seek professional help. A support group would be beneficial not only to you but to your whole family. Some are geared toward a sibling's loss and others are for parents who have lost children. As you are working through your grief, find ways to remember your brother. Make a memory book of the life and times you both shared. Most importantly treasure the time you had together.

• • • •

SEARCHING FOR THE RIGHT WORDS

••••

DEAR BARB:

A co-worker of mine lost his eighteen-year-old son in a terrible car accident. Everyone in the office was devastated and we didn't know what to say to him when he returned to work after a week off. We don't want to make the father's pain worse, but we also want to express how we feel.

Some people in the office feel we should just act as if nothing happened and others feel we should say something, but no one knows exactly what we should do or say. We need some advice. Thanks, Jeff.

••••

HI JEFF:

The loss of a child is unimaginable. No parent ever imagines that their child will die before them; it's just not the natural order of life. There is nothing you can say to make their loss any easier, but there are things you can say to let someone know that you care deeply and are concerned about their well-being. People often think it's best to say nothing, but it is better to say something. They lost a child, it's not like you are bringing something to their attention that they don't know. It's like the elephant in the room; you need to acknowledge the loss. Even saying "sorry for your loss" is an acknowledgment that you are recognizing they are in pain. Simply saying that there are no words that could make their pain any less is deeply appreciated.

Many sympathy cards may help to express the words you are unable to. Don't say you know how they feel unless you have lost a child and even then, grief is an individual experience. Don't say things like, "At least you've still got another child" even if they have another child, to say that is a no-no. The loss of one child cannot be replaced with another. Make a casserole, I know that seems like old school, but for many people, food is an expression of love and caring. Don't expect your co-worker to get over the loss of their child. Grieving a child lasts a lifetime, we learn to go on, but the loss of a child never ends.

My best advice is to not be afraid to talk about the loss. If your co-worker brings it up, engage him, allow him to express his loss, and be there to support him. A great book for a grieving parent is: *Beyond Tears: Living After Losing a Child, Revised Edition* by Ellen Mitchell. It is available in paperback on amazon.ca. As well you can also write down the title and insert it in a sympathy card, this way the parents can choose whether they want to purchase it or not. Some people find comfort in reading and some people don't. Hope this information is helpful.

• • • •

MISSING MOM

• • • •

DEAR BARB:

I am in my early thirties and have been having a hard time since my mother died. She was diagnosed with breast cancer about 10 years ago and went through treatment. Fortunately, she was well for a long time. Suddenly the cancer came back and the doctor said there was nothing more they could do for her. Even though our family had lived with the possibility of this happening, I guess I never really thought it would end like this.

My dad seems to be coping better than anybody else. It has only been nine months since mom died and he's already been on a date with another woman. I find it tough to see him with another woman. I just don't think I will ever be able to get over this grief. I can't stop thinking of all the things I will miss with my mother, like my wedding and my future children. I really need some advice. – Nancy

• • • •

HI NANCY:

Losing a parent at any age can be traumatic. No matter what the circumstances we can never be prepared to lose someone. On the other hand, as our parents age, we have more time to adjust to the inevitable. Even though you and your family were living with your mother's cancer, she was able to survive for quite a while and as you say seemed to be well. Therefore, it would be easy to convince yourself she was going to beat it.

Perhaps because you were so young when your mother became ill you didn't fully understand her prognosis, whereas your father was probably more involved with her treatment and more aware of what was happening. I know it bothers you to see your father with someone else, but would your mother have wanted him to be alone for the rest of his life? Probably not.

Grief is very personal, and people experience it in unique ways. You need to give yourself time to heal. Your mother will always be with you, as you are a part of each other. Sometimes it helps to speak to others who have experienced similar circumstances. My suggestion is to talk with your family doctor about joining a support group in your area or perhaps see a grief counselor.

Try to remember the good times you shared with your mother. I know this is going to sound like a cliché, but time heals all wounds.

• • • •

APPRECIATING DIFFERENCES

• • • •

DEAR BARB:

I was married previously, and my husband of ten years passed away after a brief illness. We had a great marriage and loved each other very much. He believed women should be spoiled and treated special. The problem is that my present husband (of three years) does not share this philosophy and so he treats me differently. For example, my first husband opened car doors for me and always tended to my needs before his own. Whereas my present husband takes care of himself first and feels it is not necessary to do things like open doors etc. I am having a hard time accepting this and we often argue about it. He says I should stop comparing him to my late husband.

Am I wrong to expect the same treatment as I had previously? What do you think? Thanks, S.T.

• • • •

HI S.T.:

Interesting question. Each person is unique and therefore treats people in their own way, however, if you do not feel loved by your present husband that could create a lot of problems within your marriage. Perhaps you need to learn to accept him for who he is and possibly modify your expectations. Strive to appreciate the fact that you were fortunate to have experienced what you had with your late husband and move on.

In time you will come to a place where you will see your present husband's expression of love as unique to him, and not compare him to your late husband. Thanks for your letter.

• • • •

OBTAINING CLOSURE

• • • •

DEAR BARB:

Within the last few years, I have had a few friends and family members pass away and two of them did not have a funeral or even a memorial service. Is this the new trend? It's like they were here one day and gone the next and I never even had a chance to say goodbye. I hope this is not the way of the future. I can see where someone wouldn't want the traditional funeral with the mass and everything, but a little memorial service is a nice way to give people closure and honor the person who passed.

What is your feeling on this issue? - Barbara M.

• • • •

HI BARBARA:

Great question. Traditional funerals are changing with the baby boomer generation. We were the generation that changed everything, so why not change the way we say goodbye? In a lot of cases, funerals are being replaced by personalized memorial services. People want to say goodbye to their loved ones in a special way and they are leaving their instructions. Many people prefer a celebration of their life when they pass rather than the sad goodbyes of yesterday. With medical advances, people are living longer and for the most part have enjoyed a long and happy life, providing time for them to make peace with their death.

So, Barbara, you are going to have to respect the wishes of the dead and find your way to achieve the closure you need. Perhaps writing a goodbye letter to the person or getting together with a couple of mutual friends or family members and sharing special stories would be helpful.

• • • •

TALKING ABOUT LOSS

• • • •

DEAR BARB:

A very dear family member recently died, and his death was a traumatic event for the entire family. The day following the death, a close friend of mine dropped by. As soon as she came in I told her about the death; she said she had heard about it, and then continued talking about herself and things that were happening in her life.

While she was talking, I could feel the anger inside of me getting ready to erupt. I was waiting for her to ask how I was, or lend a caring ear, but neither happened. She carried on for almost an hour until I said I had somewhere to go. As she was leaving, she said we should get together soon and that was it.

Why are some people like that? I wasn't up to listening to the trivial events going on in her life when our family was experiencing such a devastating loss. How can a person be so self-centered? - Frustrated in B.C.

• • • •

DEAR FRUSTRATED:

Grief is difficult for some people to deal with; they just don't know what to say, so they talk about what they know best. They may think they are helping you by distracting you and talking about themselves and their family, but, most people want to talk about their loss. Grieving people need to be heard and understood, which your friend was not able to do. You could come right out and tell your friend that you would like to talk about what happened. If she sees that you can talk, then hopefully she will listen and allow you time to express your grief.

Another option would be to go to a funeral home or check out some online sites and pick up a Guide to Dealing with Grief and give one to your friend. You can also download free brochures that may help[1]. Sorry for your loss.

1. http://www.leukemiabmtprogram.org/patients_and_family/other_resources/free_materials_for_download/information_brochures/coping_with_loss_grief.html

PART 11 - CHRISTMAS - "Christmas isn't just a day it's a frame of mind." - VALENTINE DAVIES (MIRACLE ON 34TH STREET)

BAH HUMBUG

••••

DEAR BARB:

It's almost Christmas and I just can't get into the spirit. I can't find anything to celebrate. Everybody spends too much money, eats too much food, and drinks too much alcohol. Every year somebody in my family becomes angry because somebody didn't visit them, but instead went to visit another sister or brother, or they don't like the food, Blah Blah Blah!

My parents are getting older, and I wish this would stop and we could all be together. I'm just tired of the whole thing. How does someone who feels the way I do get into the Christmas spirit? Bah humbug! Craig

••••

MERRY CHRISTMAS CRAIG!

Many individuals share your sentiments. For plenty of people, Christmas reminds them of what they don't have, as well as the people and relationships they have lost. Christmas can be especially difficult for seniors and people on fixed incomes. They don't have the extra money for gifts, specialty foods, etc. They often spend Christmas alone, without family members because of age or their inability to visit family and friends who are far away.

There are still many people who celebrate the spiritual/religious aspect of Christmas, as evidenced by the number who frequent churches on Christmas day, although there seem to be fewer people doing this nowadays. Others view Christmas as a time to reconnect with friends and family that they may not have seen for a long time. The bottom line is that Christmas is what you choose to make it.

I agree Christmas has become too commercialized. Parents spend tons of money giving their children mountains of toys that they probably will never play with. Frequently, Christmas debts last long after Christmas is over. And with interest charges, people end up paying twice as much as the gifts originally cost. It does get out of control.

All I can suggest, Craig, is for you to find your way of celebrating the holidays. Try not to get caught up in commercialism. If you can't afford to buy a gift, then don't (and don't use credit to pay for gifts). If someone cares about you, they will accept what you give and be happy to spend time with you.

Also, don't become a victim of the social politics of the day. Spend time with the family members you want to. If you cannot all be together, try to spend a little time visiting each family.

Although Christmas should be a joyous occasion, I agree the day has lost a lot of its meaning. Try to enjoy the day and thanks for writing.

SURPRISE DINNER GUEST

DEAR BARB:

Merry Christmas! I am gay and in my early twenties. I recently came out to my family, and they reacted better than I thought. Although my dad seems a little distant, my mom is pretty good with it. I am one of three siblings. My brother and sister are married with children. My parents always host Christmas dinner with all the trimmings. I am looking forward to coming home for Christmas as I live a two-hour drive away. My partner and I have been together for almost a year and I am thinking of bringing him home for Christmas to meet the family. I haven't told my parents about Derrick yet, so I'm not sure if I should bring him home. I haven't seen my parents since I told them that I am gay, but I have talked to them on chat and FaceTime. I told my sister about my relationship, but she didn't have an opinion about whether I should bring Derrick home. I don't want to cause stress for my family, but I would like to include my partner. I'd be interested in hearing your opinion on this issue. Thanks, Dan.

HI DAN:

Merry Christmas to you as well. Since you recently came out to your parents, it will probably take a while for them to feel comfortable with it, especially if they didn't have any idea you were gay. When looking back, most parents will admit that they had an inkling their child was gay from an early age, but now that it's out in the open things will change. There are other family members, such as grandparents, aunts, and uncles that will have to be told. I don't think it would be a good idea to come home with your boyfriend right now, even though you want to.

My suggestion would be to talk to your parents and see if they are open to meeting your partner before Christmas. After the meeting ask them how they would feel about you bringing Derrick home to meet the family. If they are reluctant, give them some time to adjust. This is a significant adjustment to their lives, as they most likely had a vision of how their life would unfold, and that has all changed with this new reality. Remember they are from a generation where gays stayed in the closet and people lived their lives in denial. On the other hand, they may surprise you and be open and receptive to your partner joining the family for Christmas. Good luck Dan, happy to hear you are living your truth.

• • • •

FINANCIAL STRAIN OF CHRISTMAS

• • • •

DEAR BARB:

Christmas is over and the Christmas bills are starting to roll in. I didn't realize I had spent so much money, even though I was trying to control my spending this year. It's so frustrating. I had a great Christmas, but the feeling is being spoiled by all these bills. I would like to find a way to avoid this from happening next year. I know it's early to start thinking about next Christmas, but I don't want to leave it to the last minute again. I know I should save money ahead, but I can't seem to accomplish that. Do you have any suggestions on how I could save some money for Christmas without affecting my day-to-day living, as I do not have a lot of extra money? Thanks, Jenna.

• • • •

HI JENNA:

I'm sure there are a lot of people feeling like you are right now. We all get caught up in the Christmas spirit and end up spending more than we should. The malls are filled with beautiful things that we know our loved ones would like and the stores make it so simple to make purchases. Also, credit is so easy to get, and most offer some sort of plan to defer payments. The "buy now and pay later" philosophy is way too appealing for most of us. We all think the money will somehow materialize when the payment becomes due. Unfortunately, if that does not happen, we end up with debt and monthly payments along with exorbitant interest charges. Plus, many credit cards have a yearly fee beginning at around $20 and upwards of $100. However, you can shop around and find many credit cards with no annual fees and even somewhere you can earn points that add up over the year, providing you with a nice little rebate cheque that you can use for Christmas shopping.

There is no way around it if you don't want to go into debt for Christmas; you have to begin budgeting now. Start by deciding who you are going to buy for and what type of gift they would like. Make a list and beside each name write down how much you want to spend on that person. Throughout the year watch for sales of these items and when possible, purchase the items at the sale price. Be sure that you can pay for each item when you buy it, or if you put it on your credit card make sure you pay the balance off at the end of the month. Keep track of how much you are spending on each person and if you are spending less than you budgeted, apply the extra to someone else's gift, or save it for Christmas incidentals like wrapping paper or cards. Good luck Jenna, thanks for writing about this important topic.

• • • •

I HATE CHRISTMAS

• • • •

DEAR BARB:

I hate Christmas! I know I shouldn't because "it's the happiest time of the year" but I do. I hate the money I have to spend on people I rarely see. I am already living pay cheque to pay cheque so I have to go into debt for Christmas! If I'm lucky I will get these gifts paid off before they all come back for more gifts next Christmas. I have been the lucky one who was nominated to be the host of Christmas dinner again this year. Thankfully my wife doesn't hate Christmas as much as I do. Oh, and I just can't wait to see all my family, who fortunately I haven't seen since last Christmas, which by the way, turned into a big fiasco!

My sister arrived with some guy who no one had met, with his two kids in tow. Since I didn't know about the kids coming, I had to find a couple of twenties and put them in an envelope, so they wouldn't feel left out. My other sister's husband had just left her, no doubt he's an asshole. She spent Christmas day depressed and trash-talking him to anyone who would listen. My mother is in the early stages of dementia and my dad had just been diagnosed with cancer. Unfortunately, my dad passed away six months later. Mom is still here. Sometimes. So, what's to be happy about? I think about all the poor souls who have no one at Christmas. They have no one all year, but all the build-up to Christmas just makes it seem that much worse.

Religion is not a part of Christmas anymore, so what does the day mean anyway. To me it's a day to get together with family members I would rather not see, buy gifts I can't afford, and have a meal that no one appreciates. My question is does anybody truly enjoy Christmas anymore? Thanks for allowing me to vent. – Michael

• • • •

WHOA, MICHAEL!

No doubt your story is a sad one, but you are not alone, many people are feeling the way you do about Christmas. My advice to you would be to change your thinking. Rather than seeing everything as a negative, try to see the positives. Since you are the host, you will be setting the stage for the day. When things start to turn negative with your sister, turn it around or change the subject. She will get the hint and I'm sure others will follow your lead. Sadly, your mother has dementia, but on the bright side, she is still with you, as many other people's mothers are not. You and your family can make this a special Christmas for her, as you said she is still aware at times, so make the best of those times.

Religion is still a part of Christmas; it is people who are not celebrating the true meaning of Christmas. If you believe in the religiosity of Christmas, then return the focus of your day to celebrating the birth of Christ. Make the best of this Christmas and begin to change things up for next Christmas. Talk to your family members and, if you cannot afford gifts for everyone, don't buy them. You should not have to go into debt for Christmas. Draw names and put a limit on the amount to spend on each gift, this way everyone has a gift, and no one is left out.

Do not allow yourself to be pressured into hosting Christmas dinner, take turns with your siblings. The only way things will change is if everyone in your family communicates how they feel. The alternative is to continue year after year with the same scenario and feeling the same resentment and frustration. Merry Christmas to you and your family Michael and thanks for sharing your story.

••••

CHRISTMAS HAT

••••

DEAR BARB:

Christmas is quickly approaching, and I feel the anxiety building. My family is stressing about who is going to do Christmas dinner and at whose house. I have tried to get my family to skip Christmas presents since we are all adults, but they wouldn't agree. My younger sister still wants gifts as does my brother. My parents are older and living on a fixed income, so they really can't afford to buy gifts for everyone.

I would like to keep my Christmas stress to a minimum this year; do you have any suggestions that I could use to stop the stress before it escalates? Thanks, Tammy.

• • • •

HEY TAMMY:

You're right about Christmas approaching way too quickly. Every year families stress out about the same things, and every year they end up doing the same thing over and over.

To minimize your Christmas stress, you have to identify what is causing the stress and change that situation. For example, make gift-giving easier by putting names in a hat and having everyone choose one, alternate who will be hosting Christmas dinner: begin with the oldest sibling and each year move to the next. It looks like you're going to be the one who implements this initially.

You will meet some resistance but persevere and eventually, everyone will realize their stress is reduced and they are enjoying the true meaning of Christmas, which is to get together with family. Merry Christmas Tammy.

PART 12 - PETS - "We can judge the heart of a man by his treatment of animals." - IMMANUEL KANT

••••

WHEN TO SAY GOODBYE TO KITTY

••••

DEAR BARB:

I have a cat that I love tremendously. She is nineteen years old and seems to be in a lot of pain. I am struggling with deciding when is the right time to put her down. She is still eating well and does respond to me, it's just that she appears to be in a lot of pain when she walks, and she has a pronounced limp. My vet suggested we put her on a heavy narcotic. I tried that once, but she was so strung out and paranoid that I didn't want to put her through that again.

I wish she would just pass away in her sleep so I would not have to make this decision. I don't know what to do! – Cara

••••

DEAR CARA:

Nineteen years is quite a long time for a cat to live, you must have been providing her with excellent care. You are in a situation where all pet owners will eventually find themselves. Unfortunately, there is no easy answer. The most important consideration is whether your cat is getting some enjoyment from her life. As you say she is eating well, so she is obtaining some gratification from mealtime. Also, if she is enjoying the attention you provide, then she is also receiving pleasure from her interaction with you. As far as her pain level, I think you are the only one who can determine how bad it is, as you are with her every day. Ask yourself if she has more bad days than good days. If she reaches a point where she can't stand up or use her litter, then the situation is quite serious.

Undoubtedly it is a difficult decision to make, but you are the only one who can make it. I've heard it said that concerning euthanatizing a pet, it is better to be a week early than a week late. Thanks for your important question Cara and best of luck.

····

SECOND THOUGHTS ABOUT TASHA

····

DEAR BARB:

Hi, I recently put my dog down and now I'm wondering if I did the right thing. Tasha was a ten-year-old miniature schnauzer with lots of health issues. For the last two years, she was on several expensive medications, and they were not making a difference in the quality of her life. When I asked my vet whether it was time, he said he didn't want to influence my decision; however, I finally got him to tell me what he would do if Tasha was his dog. He said he would probably put her down.

One cold snowy morning last week I took her out for her morning walk, and she just stood there shaking, even though she had a sweater on. I began to doubt whether she would be able to make it through the winter, so I took her in. At the time it felt like it was the right decision, but a week later, I'm having second thoughts. How do I resolve those conflicted feelings within myself?
– Pat

• • • •

HI PAT:

The decision to put a pet down is very difficult and many people agonize over when is the right time. We love our pets like members of our family. We don't want to see them suffer, but we also don't want to lose them. Remember that when you decided to put her down you believed it was the right thing to do. It's only after the fact that you are having second thoughts as the good memories are replacing the painful days at the end of Tasha's life. It has only been a short time since putting her down, and, although you will always grieve, you will eventually learn to live with the loss.

Fortunately, there are things you can do to help make the transition to life without your dear pet. Create a memory box with your pet's collar, favorite toy, and sweater. Take the time to create a scrapbook with all your special memories. Talk to other family members and share stories about Tasha. Check online for support groups in your area or counselors that deal specifically with pet loss. Donate to your local shelter in your pet's name. Give yourself time to grieve, everyone grieves differently.

PET SITTER TAKES A FEW NIPS

DEAR BARB:

My problem has to do with a dog sitter that I hired to look after my two poodles. My husband and I initially considered putting them in a kennel, but after touring a few, we decided our dogs would not do well. We felt it would be too traumatic for them to adjust at their age, especially with the noise and commotion in a kennel. Then we thought we had found the perfect answer. DogVacay.com is a service where people care for dogs in their homes. We set up a meet and greet with a couple of people and chose one. We brought our dogs for a trial visit for half a day just to see how things would go. One of our dogs did great, the other one shook the whole time and wouldn't eat or drink. We tried a few more times and even overnight and Ginger would not eat or drink. Needless to say, we had to find another situation.

A friend of mine recommended someone that they knew. This is a very good friend whom I have known for years, so I contacted the person she recommended. The pet sitter came over to meet the dogs on three occasions and seemed very capable. Both dogs appeared comfortable with her. So, we thought we would attempt an overnight visit. To begin with, she was 40 minutes late arriving, but I thought, "Well, no big deal." That evening, I got three or four silly emails from her, but thought she just wanted to keep me up to date. When we arrived home the next day the house was dark, and she was getting up from lying on the sofa and said she was resting. When I got close to her, I could smell alcohol.

Then I asked her how the bed downstairs was, and she said she had a couple of glasses of wine and fell asleep on the sofa. I said oh did you bring some wine, she said no I drank yours. I was shocked but didn't say anything. My husband said she should have known by the look on my face I was not happy. I had an unopened box of wine in my fridge that she opened and generously helped herself to. Everyone I tell this to gets a good laugh out of it. I would never hire her again; I think what she did was uncouth! What is your opinion? – Victoria

• • • •

HI VICTORIA:

Quite an unfortunate series of events! Yes, I do think that was impolite to open someone's wine and help yourself. I would have expected her to apologize once she saw your reaction, but since she didn't, she obviously didn't see anything wrong with what she did. You could talk to her about it and see what kind of response you get.

If you are convinced, she is sorry and won't do it again, you could try another overnight and see how it goes. On the other hand, she may feel you should provide her with alcohol. Then I think you already know what you need to do. Thanks, Victoria for sharing your interesting story.

Don't miss out!

Visit the website below and you can sign up to receive emails whenever Barbara Godin publishes a new book. There's no charge and no obligation.

https://books2read.com/r/B-A-EPYK-YSFGB

BOOKS 2 READ

Connecting independent readers to independent writers.

Also by Barbara Godin

Words of Wisdom
Dear Barb 2: Advice for Daily Life

Standalone
Dear Barb: Answers to Your Everyday Questions
Glimpses in Time: A Collection of Memoirs and More
Can I Come HOME Now?
Seasons of the Heart
Maya's Journey & Maria's Dream
Christmas Stories: Five Short Stories For Everyone

About the Author

Barbara Godin is a bestselling author, poet, and advice columnist whose work resonates deeply with readers seeking hope, healing, and connection. Her memoir, Can I Come HOME Now?, a #1 Bestseller, chronicles her journey of overcoming abuse and neglect to reclaim her life, inspiring countless readers to rise above their own challenges. Barbara's latest poetry collection, Seasons of the Heart, captures the beauty and complexity of human emotion, while her Words of Wisdom series, drawn from her beloved "Dear Barb" columns, offers practical guidance and heartfelt insights. A graduate with a B.A. in English, Barbara's writing blends raw honesty with lyrical grace. When not crafting stories or advice, she enjoys walking, hiking, biking, and spending quiet moments with her cherished cat. Through her words, Barbara continues to touch hearts and illuminate the resilience of the human spirit.

www.ingramcontent.com/pod-product-compliance
Lightning Source LLC
Chambersburg PA
CBHW070851050426
42453CB00012B/2135